A-Z WORCESTER

CONTENTS

Key to Map Pages	2-3
Large Scale Pages	4-5
Map Pages	6-42

REFERENCE

Motorway	**M5**
A Road	**A44**
B Road	**B4204**
Dual Carriageway	
One-way Street Traffic flow on A Roads is also indicated by a heavy line on the driver's left.	
Road Under Construction Opening dates are correct at the time of publication	
Proposed Road	
Restricted Access	
Pedestrianized Road	
Track / Footpath	
Residential Walkway	
Railway	Tunnel / Station / Level Crossing
Built-up Area	
Local Authority Boundary	
Posttown Boundary	
Postcode Boundary (within Posttown)	
Map Continuation	**20** / Large Scale City Centre **5**

Car Park (selected)	P
Church or Chapel	†
Cycle Route (selected)	
Fire Station	■
Hospital	H
House Numbers (A & B Roads only)	10 124
Information Centre	
National Grid Reference	405
Park & Ride	Perdiswell P+R
Police Station	▲
Post Office	★
Safety Camera with Speed Limit Fixed cameras and long term road works cameras. Symbols do not indicate camera direction.	30
Toilet: without facilities for the Disabled with facilities for the Disabled	▽ ▽
Viewpoint	
Educational Establishment	
Hospital or Healthcare Building	
Industrial Building	
Leisure or Recreational Facility	
Place of Interest	
Public Building	
Shopping Centre or Market	
Other Selected Buildings	

SCALE

Map Pages 6-42	Map Pages 4-5
1:15,840 4 inches (10.16 cm) to 1 mile 6.31 cm to 1km	1:7,920 8 inches (20.32 cm) to 1 mile 12.63 cm to 1km
0 ¼ ½ Mile	0 ⅛ ¼ Mile
0 250 500 750 Metres	0 100 200 300 Metres

Copyright of Geographers' A-Z Map Company Limited

Fairfield Road, Borough Green, Sevenoaks, Kent TN15 8PP
Telephone: 01732 781000 (Enquiries & Trade Sales)
01732 783422 (Retail Sales)

www.az.co.uk
Copyright © Geographers' A-Z Map Co. Ltd.
Edition 3 2012

 Ordnance Survey® This product includes mapping data licensed from Ordnance Survey® with the permission of the Controller of Her Majesty's Stationery Office.

© Crown Copyright 2011. All rights reserved. Licence number 100017302
Safety camera information supplied by www.PocketGPSWorld.com
Speed Camera Location Database Copyright 2011 © PocketGPSWorld.com

Every possible care has been taken to ensure that, to the best of our knowledge, the information contained in this atlas is accurate at the date of publication. However, we cannot warrant that our work is entirely error free and whilst we would be grateful to learn of any inaccuracies, we do not accept any responsibility for loss or damage resulting from reliance on information contained within this publication.

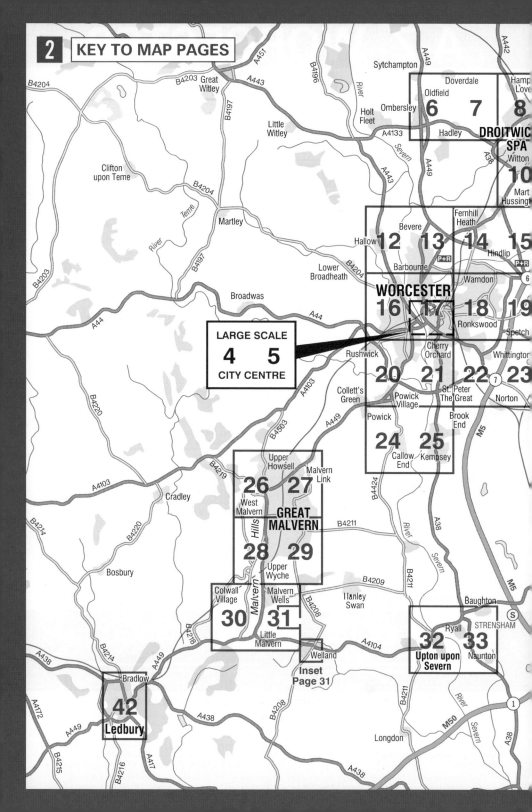

B4204

B4203 Great Witley

A443

B4196

River

Sytchampton

A4449

A442

Doverdale

Oldfield

Ombersley **6** **7** **8**

Hamp Love

DROITWIC SPA

Holt Fleet

Hadley

Witton

10

A4133

Severn

A38

A449

Mart Hussing

Little Witley

Clifton upon Teme

B4204

B4197

Fernhill Heath

Bevere

Hallow **12** **13** **14** **15**

Hindlip

Teme

Martley

River

B4197

Lower Broadheath

B4204

Barbourne

P+R

P+R

Warndon

6

Broadwas

A44

WORCESTER

16 **17** **18** **19**

Ronkswood

Spetch

LARGE SCALE

4 **5**

CITY CENTRE

Rushwick

Cherry Orchard

Whittington

A4103

B4220

B4503

A449

Collett's Green

20 **21** **22** **23**

Powick Village

St. Peter The Great

Norton

7

B4219

Powick

Brook End

M5

B4220

A4103

Cradley

Upper Howsell

Malvern Link

24 **25**

Callow End Kempsey

B4424

River

A38

B4214

West Malvern **26** **27**

GREAT MALVERN

B4211

Severn

M5

Bosbury

Hills

Malvern

28 **29**

Upper Wyche

B4209

B4211

Baughton

S

Colwall Village

Malvern Wells

30 **31**

Little Malvern

Hanley Swan

Ryall **STRENSHAM**

B4208

A4104

32 **33**

Upton upon Severn

Naunton

A4172

A438

Bradlow

B4214

A449

B4218

B4208

Welland

Inset Page 31

B4211

River

Severn

A38

1

42

Ledbury

A438

Longdon

M50

B4225

B4216

A417

A438

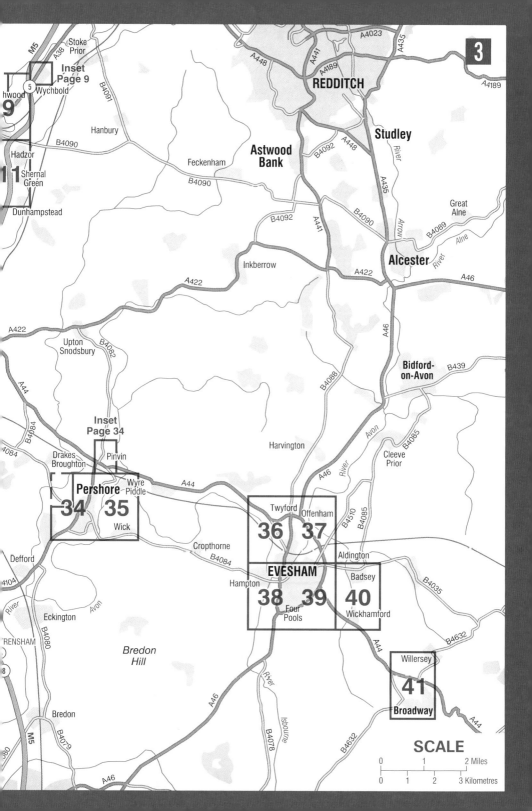

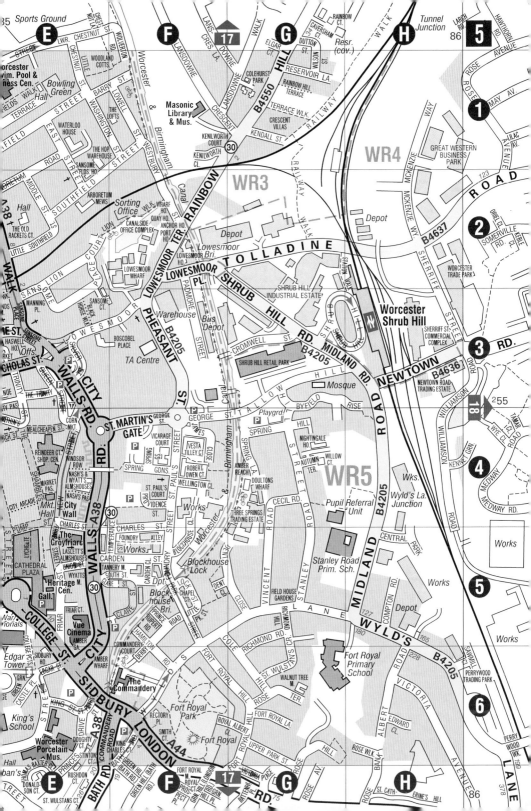

6

84

66

A Sytchampton
Pardoe's Farm
DARK LANE

Woodfield Oaks
Woodfield LANE
WOODFIELD

B Sytchampton Endowed First Sch.
Social Cen.
385

Orchard Bungalow
Oak Cottages

C

D Doverdale
Doverda Mill

Stourport-on-Severn DY13

COW LANE
CRAWFORD
A449

Elmley Brook

1

Woodfield Lodge
Woodfield Farm
NORTH- AMPTON LANE

The Orchard

Yarding's Farm

2

Oldfield
M A I N
LANE
OLDFIELD

265

Winter Nellis
The Laurels

Southview
FRUITERERS ARMS CARAVAN PARK
Mayfield House
The Firs

UPHAMPTON
LANE

Sewage Works

Dean's Wood

3

Uphampton

WOODHALL LANE
WOODHALL
WOODHALL CL.
OAKFIELD RD.
NELLINGTON CL.
SANDYS
WK.
CH.
LANE HAYE
HAYE

Arles Co
The Willows

4

OMBERSLEY
A4133
A449

RACKS LA.
The Racks

Hadley Cross House

Haye Farm

Nash Inning
64

LONGWALK
ROAD
Hall Spts. Grd.
CHAPEL LA.

Ombersley Endowed First School
SCHOOL BANK

The Cross
A4133

5

PARSONAGE LA.
WALNUT TREE CL.
APPLE TREE WK.
APPLE TREE WK.
A4133
HOLT FLEET ROAD
DROIT-WICH RD.

ROAD

Reservoir (covered)

Hadley Farm
Gardener's Grove
Orchard Cottage

Vine Cottage
War Meml.
CHURCH LA.
HILL TOP LA.

Ombersley Court

6

Ombersley Park
63

MAIN RD.
A4133
A449
DROIT-
Cricket Ground
Pav.
SINTON LA.
Sinton Farm
SINTON LA.
Moat Farm

Knight's Grove

A Black Pool
84

B
385

C

D

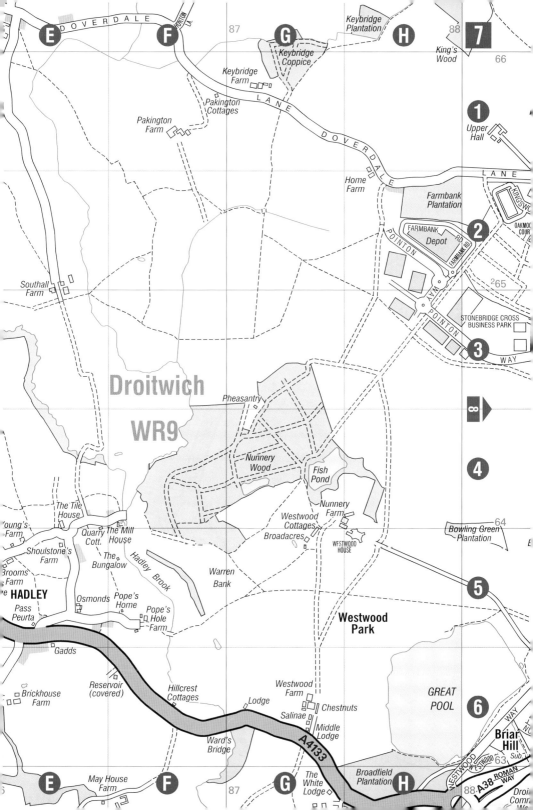

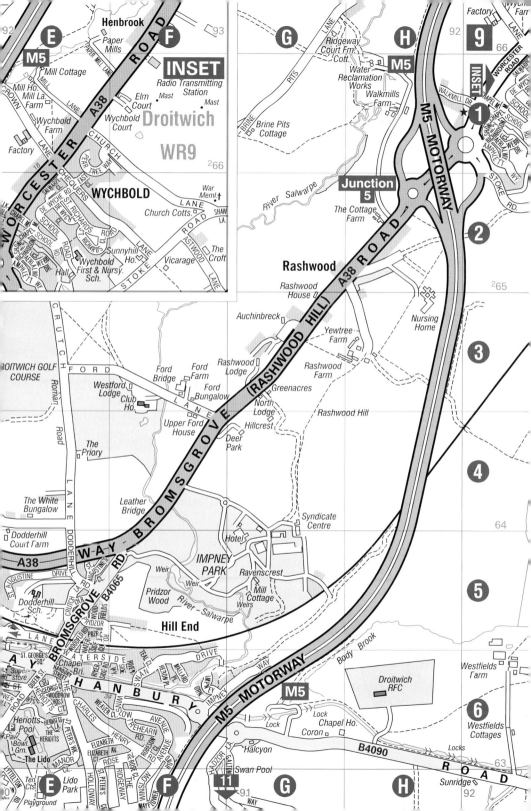

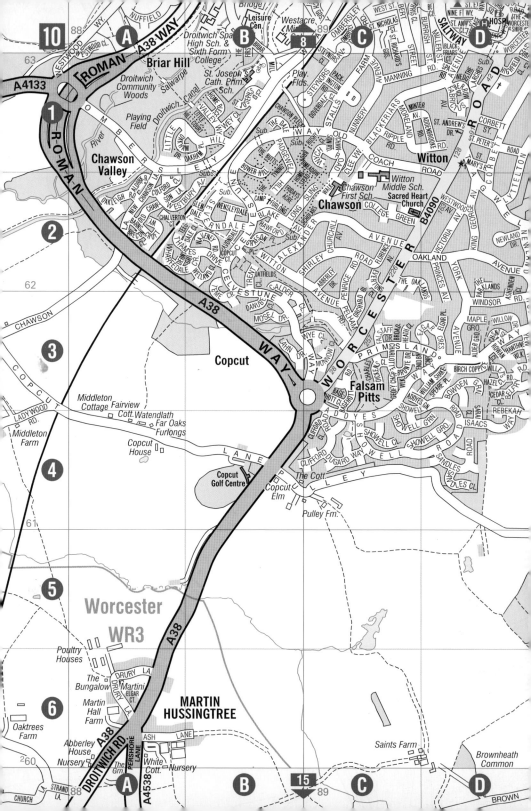

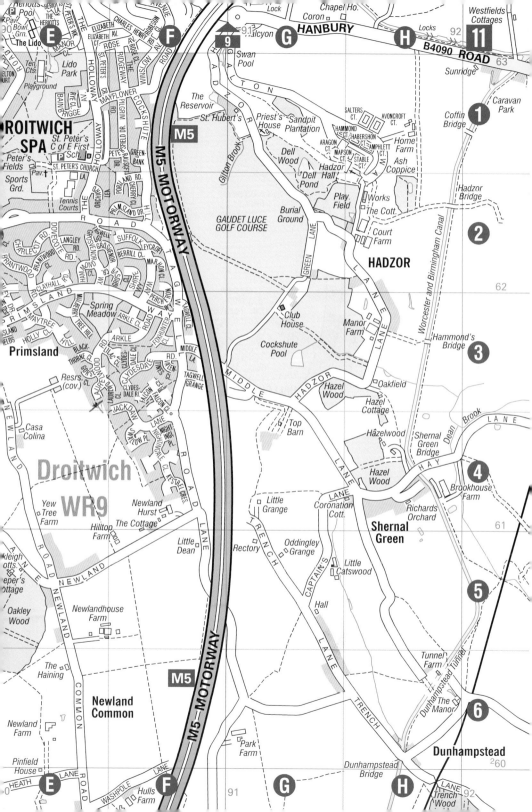

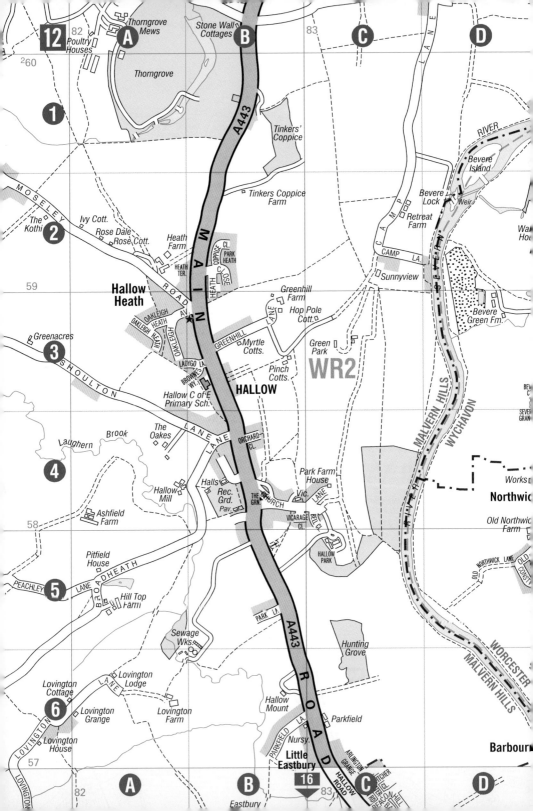

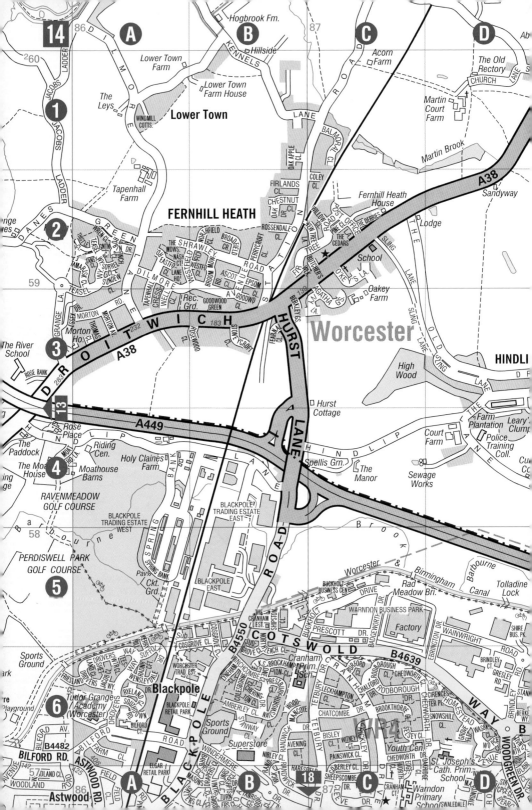

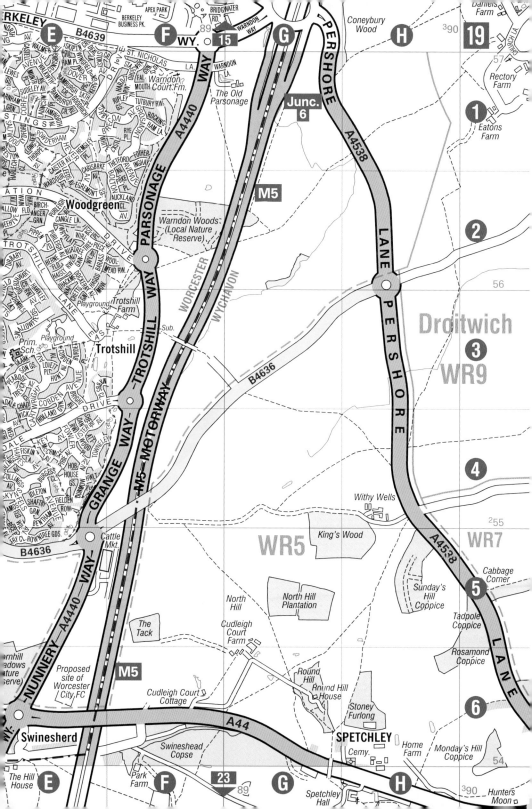

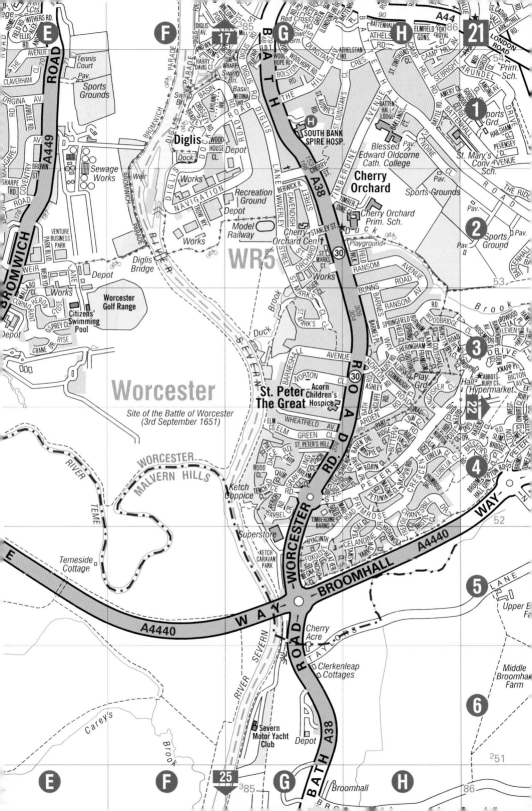

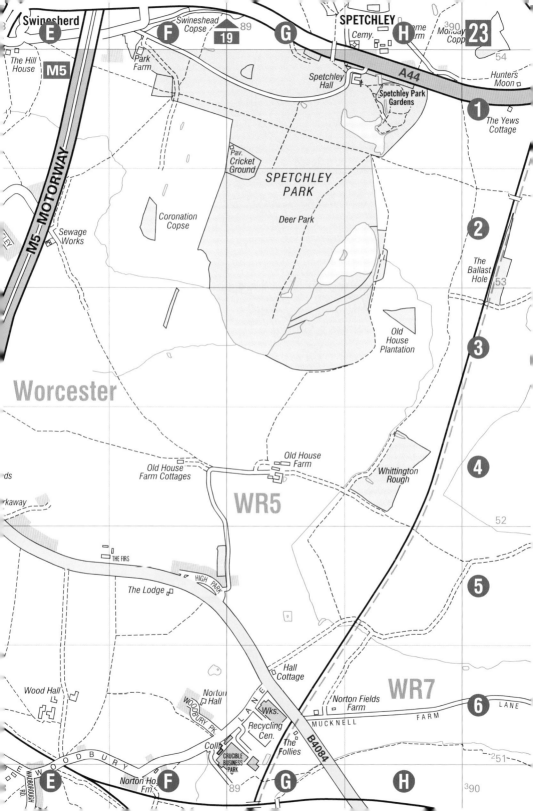

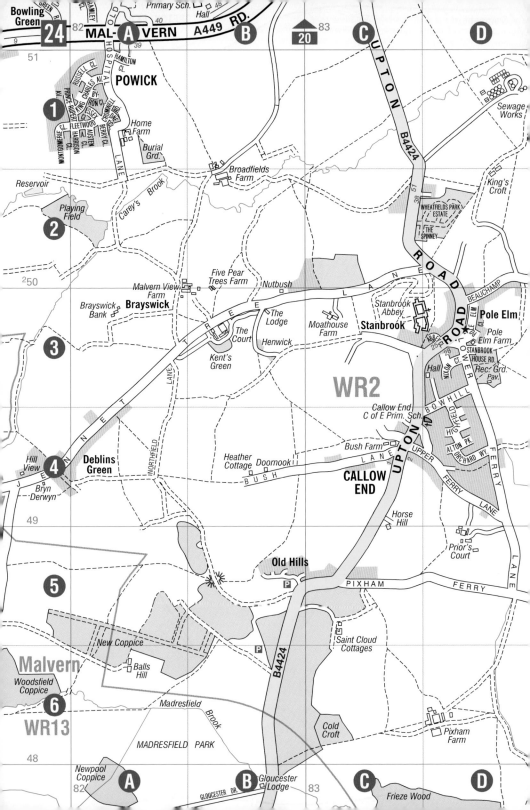

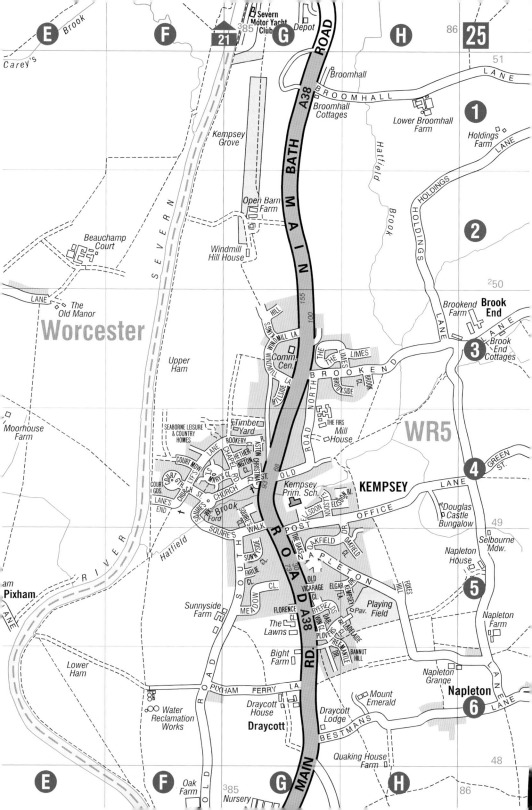

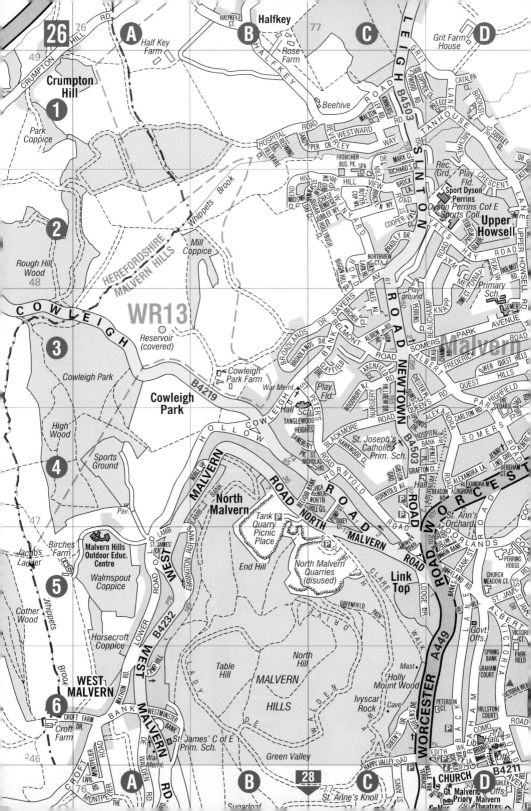

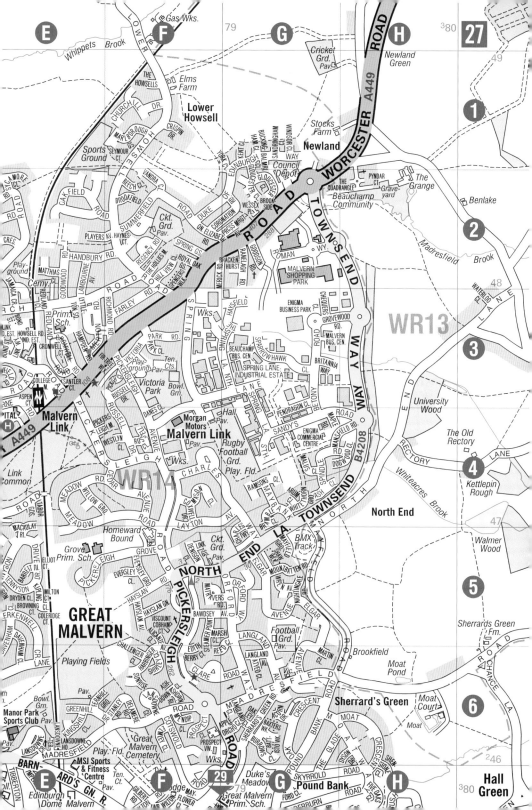

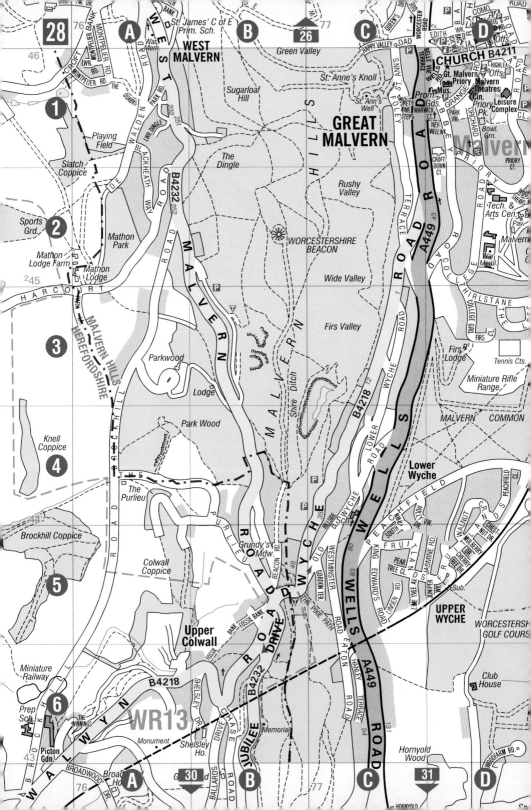

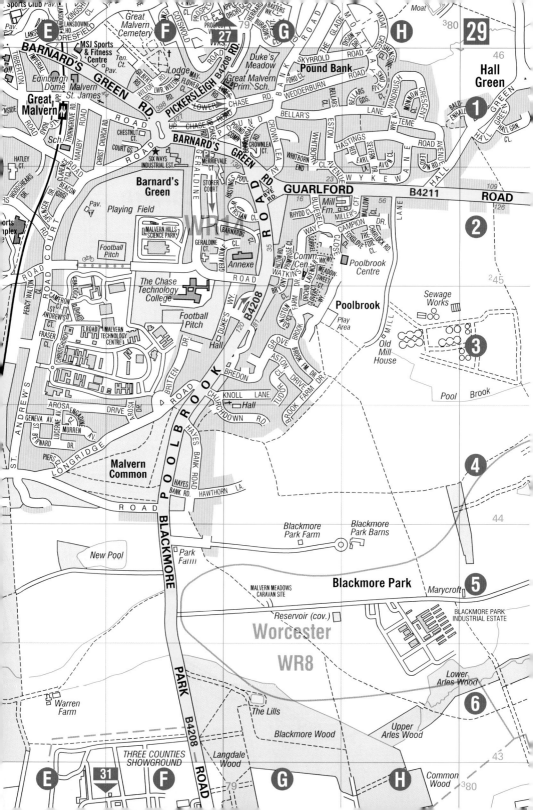

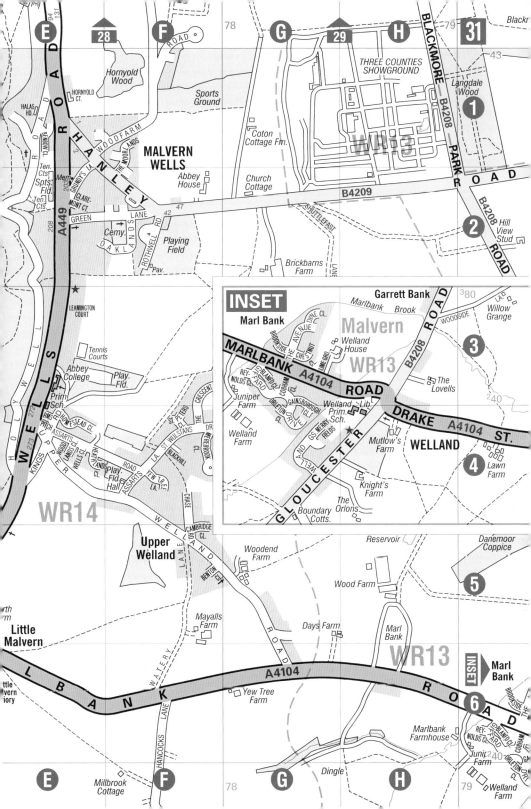

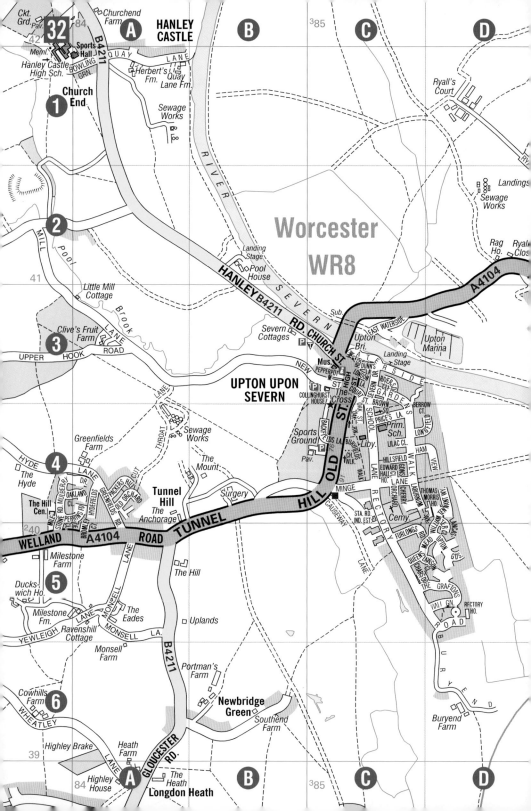

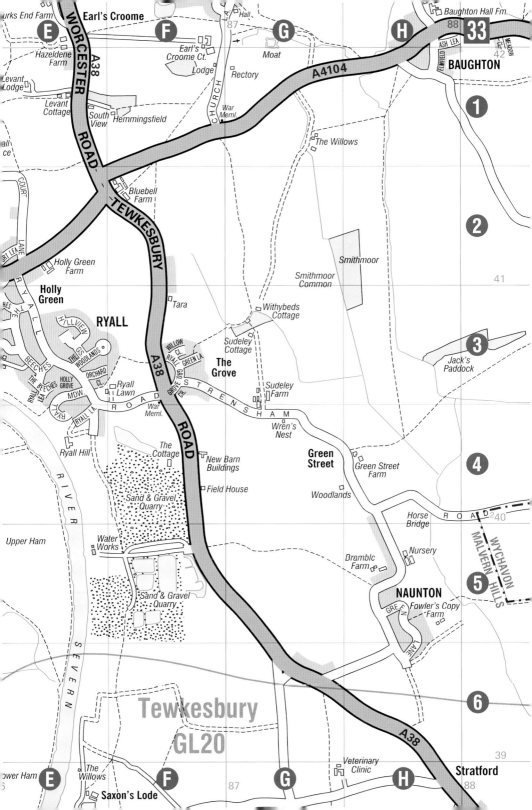

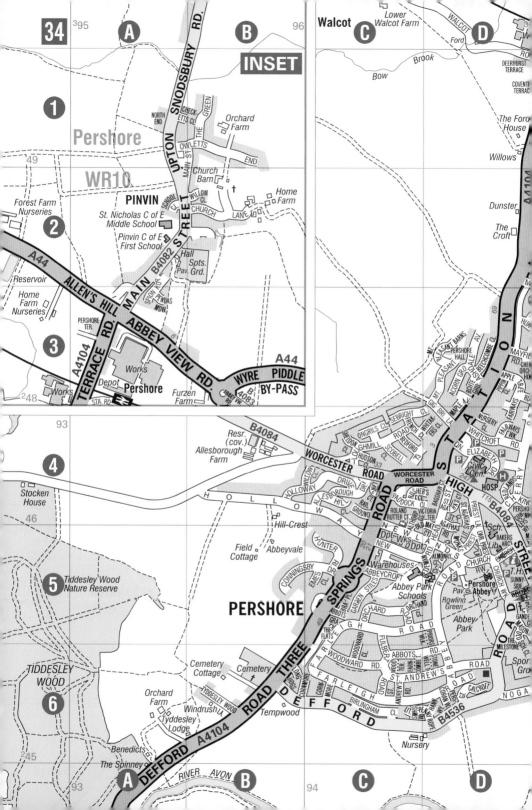

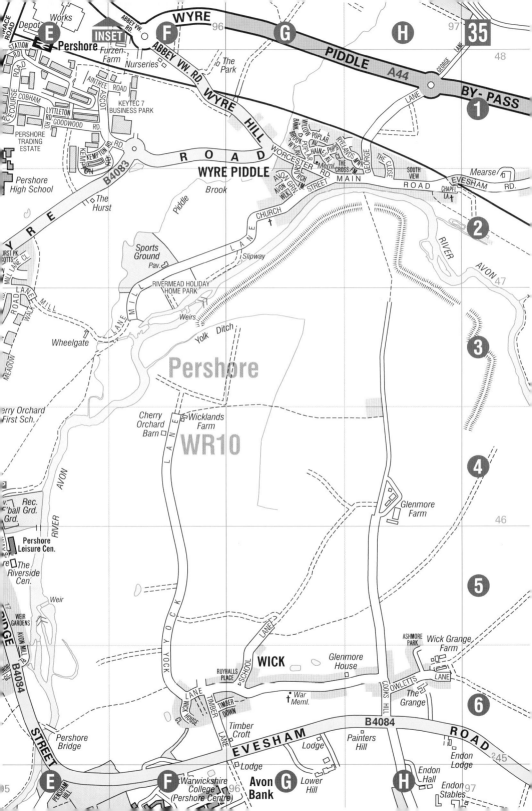

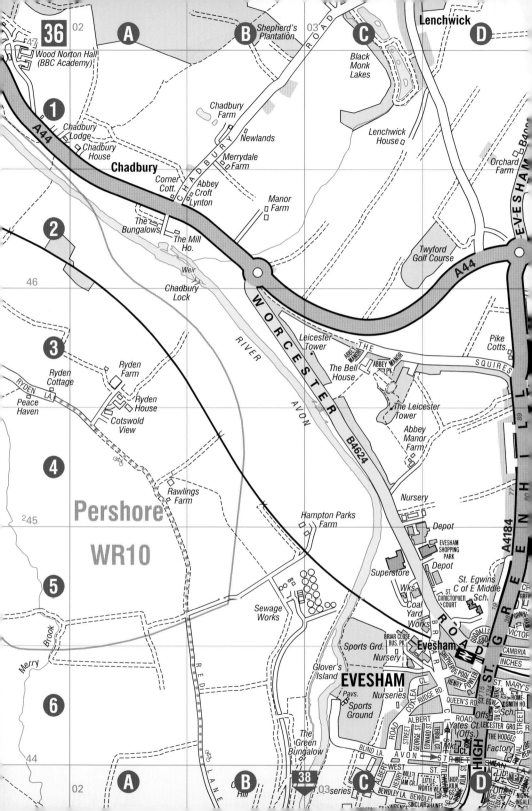

A   B   Shepherd's Plantation   03   C   D   Lenchwick

Wood Norton Hall
(BBC Academy)

1
Chadbury
Lodge
Chadbury Farm
Newlands
Chadbury
House
Chadbury
Merrydale Farm
Corner Cott.
Abbey Croft
Lynton
Manor Farm

Black Monk Lakes
Lenchwick House
Orchard Farm

2
The Bungalows
The Mill Ho.
Weir
Chadbury Lock

Twyford Golf Course
A44

46

3
Ryden Cottage
Peace Haven
RYDEN LA.
Ryden Farm
Ryden House
Cotswold View

RIVER
WORCESTER
AVON
B4624

Leicester Tower
The Bell House
ABBEY MANOR PK.
The Leicester Tower
Abbey Manor Farm

THE SQUIRES
Pike Cotts.

4
Rawlings Farm

Nursery

Pershore
WR10

2 45

Hampton Parks Farm

Depot
EVESHAM SHOPPING PARK
Depot
Superstore
St. Egwins C of E Middle Sch.

5

Sewage Works

BRIAR CLOSE BUS. PK.
Sports Grd.
Nursery
Evesham
Glover's Island

Wks
ST. CHRISTOPHER COURT
Coal Yard
Works

EVESHAM
Pavs.
Sports Ground
Nurseries

6
Merry
BROOK

The Green Bungalow

A   02   B   Hill   **38**   03 series   C   D

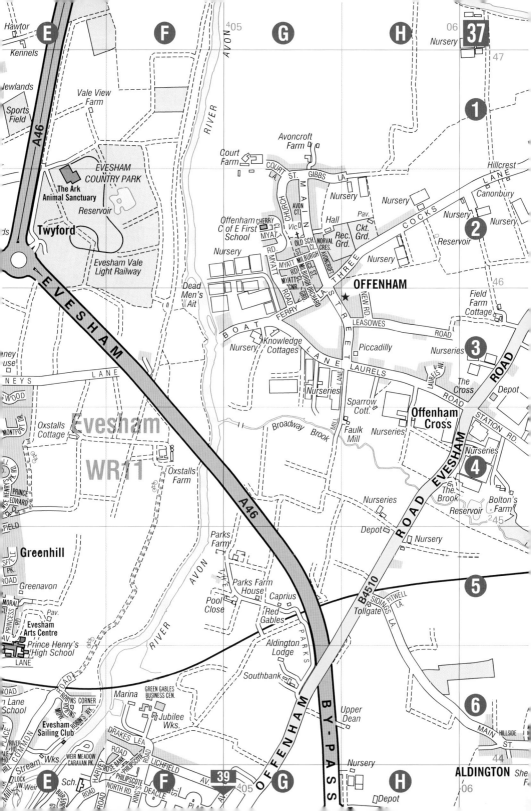

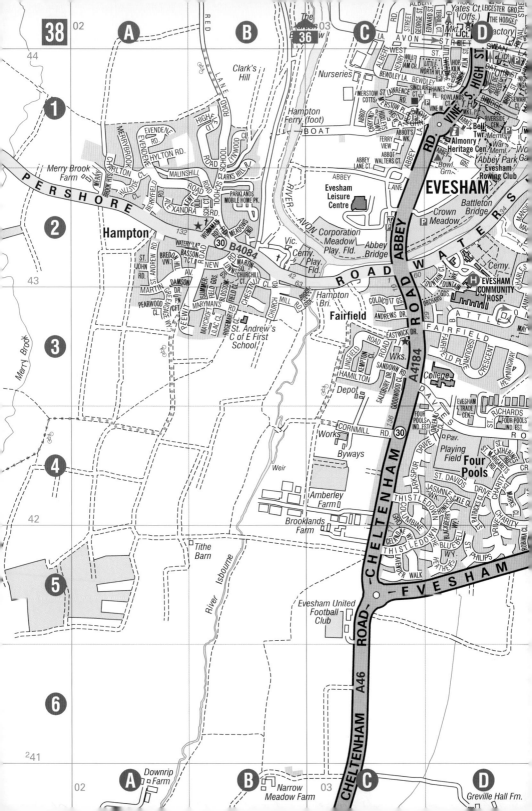

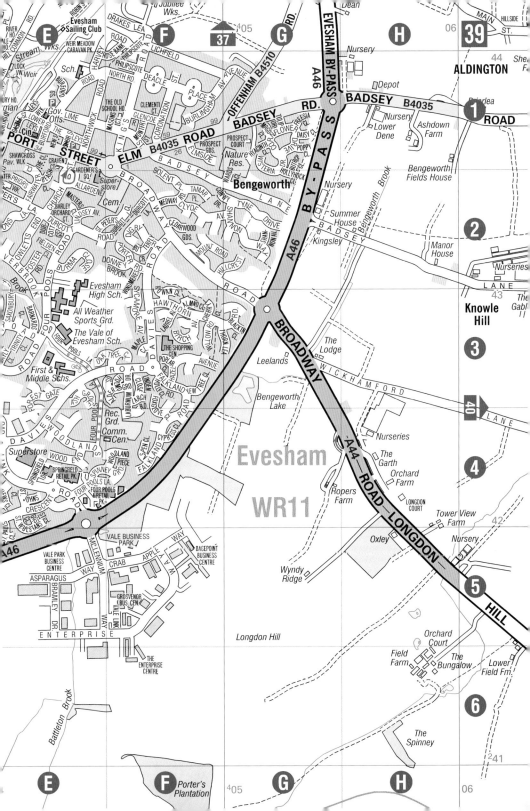

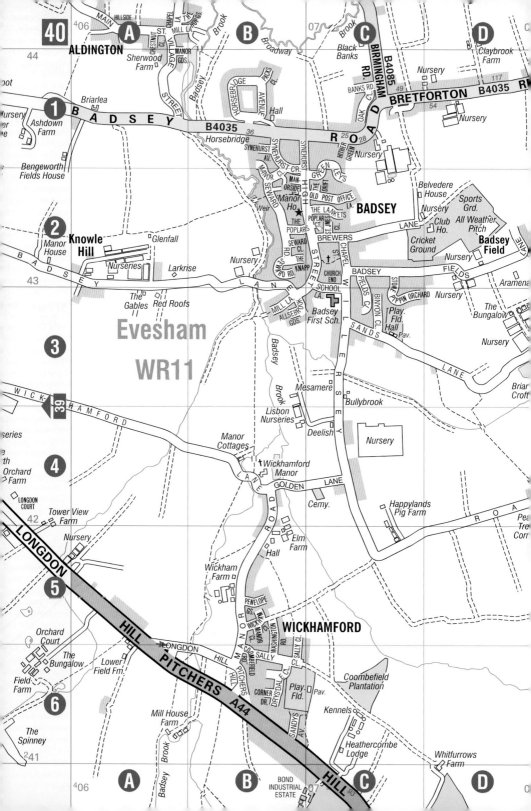

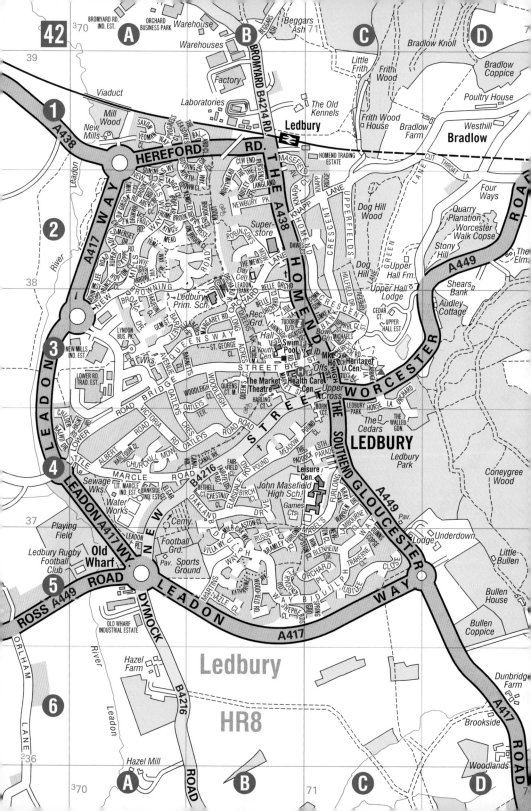

INDEX

Including Streets, Places & Areas, Hospitals etc., Industrial Estates,
Selected Flats & Walkways, Stations and Selected Places of Interest.

HOW TO USE THIS INDEX

1. Each street name is followed by its Postcode District, then by its Locality abbreviation(s) and then by its map reference;
   e.g. **Abbey Rd.** WR10: Per . . . .6D **34** is in the WR10 Postcode District and the Pershore Locality and is to be found in square 6D on page **34**.
   The page number is shown in bold type.

2. A strict alphabetical order is followed in which Av., Rd., St., etc. (though abbreviated) are read in full and as part of the street name;
   e.g. **East Waterside** appears after **Eastward Rd.** but before **Eastwick Dr.**

3. Streets and a selection of flats and walkways that cannot be shown on the mapping, appear in the index with the thoroughfare to which
   they are connected shown in brackets; e.g. **Abbey Ga.** WR11: Eves . . . .1D **38** (off Vine St.)

4. Addresses that are in more than one part are referred to as not continuous.

5. Places and areas are shown in the index in BLUE TYPE and the map reference is to the actual map square in which the town centre or area is
   located and not to the place name shown on the map; e.g. BADSEY 2B **40**

6. An example of a selected place of interest is **Malvern Mus. of Local History** 1D **28**

7. An example of a station is **Colwall Station (Rail)** . . . .2B **30**, also included is **Park & Ride**.
   e.g. **Perdiswell (Park & Ride)** 5G **13**

8. An example of a Hospital or selected Healthcare Facility is **DROITWICH SPA BMI HOSPITAL** 6D **8**

9. Map references for entries that appear on large scale pages **4** & **5** are shown first, with small scale map references shown in brackets;
   e.g. **All Saints' Rd.** WR1: Worc 4C **4** (5F **17**)

GENERAL ABBREVIATIONS

All. : Alley	**Flds.** : Fields	**Mus.** : Museum
App. : Approach	**Gdn.** : Garden	**Nth.** : North
Arc. : Arcade	**Gdns.** : Gardens	**Pde.** : Parade
Av. : Avenue	**Gth.** : Garth	**Pk.** : Park
Blvd. : Boulevard	**Ga.** : Gate	**Pas.** : Passage
Bldg. : Building	**Gt.** : Great	**Pl.** : Place
Bri. : Bridge	**Grn.** : Green	**Ri.** : Rise
Bus. : Business	**Gro.** : Grove	**Rd.** : Road
Cvn. : Caravan	**Hgts.** : Heights	**Shop.** : Shopping
Cen. : Centre	**Ho.** : House	**Sth.** : South
Chu. : Church	**Ho's.** : Houses	**Sq.** : Square
Cl. : Close	**Ind.** : Industrial	**St.** : Street
Comn. : Common	**Info.** : Information	**Ter.** : Terrace
Cnr. : Corner	**La.** : Lane	**Trad.** : Trading
Cotts. : Cottages	**Lit.** : Little	**Up.** : Upper
Ct. : Court	**Lwr.** : Lower	**Va.** : Vale
Cres. : Crescent	**Mnr.** : Manor	**Vw.** : View
Cft. : Croft	**Mkt.** : Market	**Vs.** : Villas
Dr. : Drive	**Mdw.** : Meadow	**Vis.** : Visitors
E. : East	**Mdws.** : Meadows	**Wlk.** : Walk
Est. : Estate	**M.** : Mews	**W.** : West
Fld. : Field	**Mt.** : Mount	**Yd.** : Yard

LOCALITY ABBREVIATIONS

Ald : **Aldington**	Hamp : **Hampton**	Pow : **Powick**
Dad : **Badsey**	Hamp L : **Hampton Lovett**	Rash : **Rashwood**
Bau : **Baughton**	Han C : **Hanley Castle**	R'ick : **Ruchwick**
Bev : **Bevere**	Han S : **Hanley Swan**	Rya : **Ryall**
B'ter : **Blackminster**	Harv : **Harvington**	Salw : **Salwarpe**
Brad : **Bradlow**	Hind : **Hindlip**	Sha G : **Sharnal Green**
B'way : **Broadway**	Hint G : **Hinton on the Green**	Spet : **Spetchley**
B Vill : **Brockhill Village**	Holl G : **Holly Green**	Stor : **Storridge**
C End : **Callow End**	Kemp : **Kempsey**	Stoult : **Stoulton**
Chad : **Chadbury**	Lady : **Ladywood**	S'ton : **Sytchampton**
Char : **Charlton**	Led : **Ledbury**	Tib : **Tibberton**
Clain : **Claines**	Ledd : **Leddington**	Uph : **Uphampton**
Clev : **Clevelode**	Len : **Lenchwick**	Upp C : **Upper Colwall**
C Grn : **Colwall Green**	L Mal : **Little Malvern**	Upp M : **Upper Moor**
C Sto : **Colwall Stone**	Lwr Bro : **Lower Broadheath**	Upt S : **Upton upon Severn**
Cop : **Copcut**	Lwr Moor : **Lower Moor**	Warn : **Warndon**
Crad : **Cradley**	Mad : **Madresfield**	Well : **Welland**
Dov : **Doverdale**	Mal : **Malvern**	W'ton H : **Wellington Heath**
D Bro : **Drakes Broughton**	Mal W : **Malvern Wells**	W Mal : **West Malvern**
D Spa : **Droitwich Spa**	M Hus : **Martin Hussingtree**	Westw : **Westwood**
D'tead : **Dunhampstead**	Naun : **Naunton**	Whitt : **Whittington**
E Cro : **Earl's Croome**	New : **Newland**	Wick : **Wick**
Elm : **Elmbridge**	Nort : **Norton**	W'ford : **Wickhamford**
Eves : **Evesham**	Odd : **Oddingley**	Will : **Willersey**
Fern H : **Fernhill Heath**	Off : **Offenham**	Worc : **Worcester**
Grim : **Grimley**	Omb : **Ombersley**	Wych : **Wychbold**
H'ley : **Hadley**	Park : **Parkway**	W Pid : **Wyre Piddle**
H'zor : **Hadzor**	Per : **Pershore**	
Hall : **Hallow**	Pin : **Pinvin**	

Abberley Dr.—Batten Hall Lodge

A

Abberley Dr. WR9: D Spa 2C **10**
Abberley Vw. WR3: Worc 2G **17**
Abbey Cl. WR2: C End 3D **24**
WR2: Worc 6D **16**
Abbeycroft WR10: Per 5C **34**
Abbey Gdns. WR11: Eves 1D **38**
Abbey Ga. *WR11: Eves* *1D 38*
(off Vine St.)
Abbey La. WR11: Eves 2C **38**
Abbey La. Ct. WR11: Eves 1C **38**
Abbey Mnr. WR11: Eves 3C **36**
Abbey Mnr. Pk. WR11: Eves 3C **36**
Abbey M. WR11: Eves 1D **38**
Abbey Rd. WR2: Worc 6A **4** (6D **16**)
WR10: Per 6D **34**
WR11: Eves 2C **38**
WR14: Mal 1D **28**
Abbey Vw. Rd. WR10: Pin 3A **34**
Abbot Chryton's Pl. WR11: Eves 1C **38**
Abbotsbury Ct. WR5: Worc 3A **22**
Abbots Cl. WR2: Worc 4C **16**
Abbots Grange WR10: Per 5C **34**
Abbots Rd. WR10: Per 6C **34**
Abbot's Wlk. WR11: Eves 1C **38**
Abbotswood WR11: Eves 3D **36**
Abbot Walters Ct. WR11: Eves 1C **38**
Abercrombie Cl. HR8: Led 2A **42**
Acacia Cl. WR4: Worc 2A **18**
Aconbury Cl. WR5: Worc 4D **18**
Acorn Cl. WR13: C Sto 1B **30**
Acorn Dr. WR14: Mal 6G **27**
Acorn Gro. WR10: Per 3D **34**
ACORNS CHILDREN'S HOSPICE (WORCESTER) 3G **21**
Acre La. WR9: D Spa 6C **8**
Addenbrooke Rd. WR9: D Spa 1D **10**
Addison Rd. WR3: Worc 1G **17**
Addyes Grn. WR9: D Spa 3C **10**
Addyes Way WR9: D Spa 4C **10**
Adelaide Cl. WR3: Worc 1F **17**
WR5: Kemp 5H **25**
Admiral Pl. WR5: Worc 4B **22**
Adrian Cl. WR9: D Spa 2E **11**
Aerial Way WR9: Wych 2E **9**
Agatha Gdns. WR3: Fern H 3C **14**
Aintree Rd. WR10: Per 1E **35**
Albany Rd. WR3: Worc 3H **17**
Albany Ter. WR1: Worc 1B **4** (3F **17**)
Albemarle *WR5: B Vill* *5B 22*
(off Crookbarrow Rd.)
Alberta Cl. WR2: Worc 2C **20**
Albert Pk. M. WR14: Mal 4D **26**
Albert Pk. Rd. WR14: Mal 3C **26**
Albert Rd. HR8: Led 4A **42**
WR5: Worc 6H **5** (6H **17**)
WR11: Eves 1C **38**
WR13: C Sto 2A **30**
Albert Rd. Nth. WR14: Mal 5D **26**
Albert Rd. Sth. WR14: Mal 2E **29**
Albert St. WR9: D Spa 6C **8**
Albion Mill WR1: Worc 6G **17**
Albion Rd. WR14: Mal 3C **26**
Albion Wlk. WR14: Mal 3C **26**
Alderbrook Rd. WR9: D Spa 2A **10**
Alder Cl. WR3: Worc 2H **17**
Alder Gro. WR9: D Spa 3D **10**
WR11: Eves 3F **39**
Aldersey Cl. WR5: Worc 3H **21**
Aldersey Rd. WR5: Worc 3H **21**
ALDINGTON 1A **40**
Alexander Av. WR9: D Spa 2B **10**
Alexander Rd. WR2: Worc 6E **17**
Alexandra La. WR14: Mal 4D **26**
Alexandra M. WR14: Mal 4D **26**
Alexandra Rd. WR11: Hamp 2A **38**
WR14: Mal 4D **26**
Alicante Cl. WR14: Mal 5F **27**
Allardene WR11: Eves 2E **39**
Allee de Dreux WR11: Eves 1D **38**
Allen's Hill WR10: Pin 3A **34**
Allesborough Dr. WR10: Per 4C **34**
All Saints Ho. WR1: Worc 4C **4**
All Saints' Rd. WR1: Worc 4C **4** (5F **17**)
Allsebrook Gdns. WR11: Bad 3B **40**
Alma St. WR3: Worc 1F **17**
Almond Cl. WR11: Eves 3F **39**
Almonry Cl. WR10: Per 5D **34**
Almonry Heritage Cen. 1D **38**
Althorp Gdns. WR10: Per 4C **34**
Alton Pk. WR2: C End 4D **24**
Alton Rd. WR5: Worc 4A **22**
Amber Ga. WR1: Worc 5E **5**
Amberley Cl. WR4: Warn 6B **14**
Amber Reach WR5: Worc 4G **5**
Amber Wharf WR1: Worc 6E **5** (6G **17**)
Ambleside Dr. WR4: Warn 2B **18**
Ambrose Cl. WR2: Worc 4B **16**
Amery Cl. WR5: Worc 1H **21**
Amos Gdns. WR4: Warn 4E **19**
Amphlett Ct. WR9: H'zor 1H **11**
Amphlett Way WR9: Wych 2E **9**
Amroth Gdns. WR4: Warn 6D **14**
Anchor Ho. WR1: Worc 2F **5**
Andrew Cl. WR2: Worc 3C **16**
Andrews Dr. WR11: Eves 3C **38**
Angel Cen. WR1: Worc 3D **4**
Angel Hotel *WR1: Worc* *3D 4*
(off Angel Pl.)
Angel La. WR1: Worc 4D **4** (5F **17**)
Angel Pl. WR1: Worc 3D **4** (4F **17**)
Angel Row WR1: Worc 3D **4** (4F **17**)
Angel St. WR1: Worc 3D **4** (4F **17**)
Ankerage Grn. WR4: Warn 3D **18**
Anne Cres. WR11: Eves 3D **38**
Apex Pk. WR4: Warn 6F **15**
Apple Orchard Cl. WR14: Mal 6G **27**
Apple Tree Rd. WR10: Per 3D **34**
Apple Tree Wlk. WR9: Omb 5A **6**
Aragon Ct. WR9: H'zor 1G **11**
Arboretum M. WR1: Worc 2E **5** (4G **17**)
Arboretum Rd. WR1: Worc 2E **5** (4G **17**)
Archer Cl. WR14: Mal 3C **26**
Archers Cl. WR9: D Spa 6B **8**
Arden Rd. WR5: Worc 4H **21**
Ark Animal Sanctuary, The 2E **37**
Arkle Cl. WR9: D Spa 3F **11**
Arkle Rd. WR9: D Spa 3F **11**
Arlington Grange WR2: Worc 6C **12**
Armstrong Dr. WR1: Worc 1F **21**
Arosa Dr. WR14: Mal 4E **29**
Arran Pl. WR5: Worc 3B **22**
Arrow Cft. WR9: D Spa 5C **8**
Arrowsmith Av. WR2: Worc 3A **4** (4D **16**)
Arrow Vw. HR8: Led 2A **42**
Arum Cl. WR14: Mal 4G **27**
Arundel Dr. WR5: Worc 1A **22**
Ascot Cl. WR3: Fern H 2B **14**
Ascot Rd. WR10: Per 1E **35**
Asha Ct. WR2: Worc 6A **4**
Ash Av. WR4: Worc 2A **18**
Ashby WR4: Warn 1E **19**
Ash Cl. WR14: Mal 4G **27**
Ashcroft Rd. WR1: Worc 3F **17**
Ashdale Av. WR10: Per 3D **34**
Ashdown Cl. WR2: Worc 2E **21**
WR14: Mal 6F **27**
Ashdown Ri. WR14: Mal 6F **27**
Ashenden Cl. WR9: D Spa 2D **10**
Ash Gro. WR11: Eves 3E **39**
Ashgrove WR14: Mal 4D **26**
Ash La. WR3: M Hus 6A **10**
Ash Lea WR8: Bau 1H **33**
Ashley Rd. WR5: Worc 3H **21**
Ashmore Pk. WR10: Wick 5H **35**
Asparagus Way WR11: Eves 5E **39**
Aspen Cl. WR11: Eves 4F **39**
Aspen Ct. WR14: Mal 3E **27**
Assarts La. WR14: Mal W 4F **31**
Assarts Rd. WR14: Mal W 4E **31**
Aston Cl. HR8: Led 4B **42**
WR5: Kemp 4G **25**
Aston Dr. WR14: Mal 3G **29**
ASTWOOD 1H **17**
Astwood Ct. WR3: Worc 1A **18**
Astwood La. WR9: Wych 2F **9**
Astwood Rd. WR3: Worc 6A **14**
Athelstan Ho. WR5: Worc 1H **21**
Athelstan Rd. WR5: Worc 6H **17**
Attwood Pl. WR4: Warn 4E **19**
Atyeo Cl. WR14: Mal 6G **27**
Auckland Cl. WR4: Warn 2F **19**
Auden Cres. HR8: Led 2A **42**
Audley Cft. HR8: Led 2B **42**
Austen Cl. WR2: Pow 1A **24**
Autumn Ter. WR5: Worc 4G **5** (5H **17**)
Avening Cl. WR4: Warn 6B **14**
Avenue, The WR1: Worc 3D **4** (4G **17**)
WR2: Worc 1E **21**
WR13: Well 3G **31**
Avenue Rd. WR2: Worc 6D **16**
WR14: Mal 1D **28**
Averill Cl. WR12: B'way 5G **41**
AVON BANK 6G **35**
Avon Cl. WR4: Warn 3B **18**
WR14: Mal 1H **29**
Avon Ct. WR11: Off 2G **37**
Avoncroft WR11: Off 2G **37**
Avoncroft Ct. WR9: H'zor 1H **11**
Avondale WR9: D Spa 2B **10**
Avon Grn. WR10: W Pid 2G **35**
Avon Mill Pl. WR10: Per 5E **35**
Avon Rd. WR4: Warn 3B **18**
WR10: Per 3E **35**
Avon St. WR11: Eves 6C **36**
Awford La. DY13: S'ton 1A **6**
WR9: Dov 1A **6**
Aycliffe Rd. WR5: Worc 3H **21**
Aylton Cl. WR5: Worc 1D **22**

B

Bacchurst Pl. WR4: Warn 2E **19**
Backfields La. WR8: Upt Sev 4C **32**
Back La. WR12: B'way 5F **41**
WR14: Mal 6D **26**
Back La. Nth. WR1: Worc 1B **4** (3E **17**)
Back La. Sth. WR1: Worc 2C **4** (4F **17**)
Back Wlk. WR1: Worc 1C **4** (3F **17**)
Badger Gdns. WR5: Worc 4A **22**
Badgeworth Dr. WR4: Warn 5C **14**
BADSEY 2B **40**
BADSEY FIELD 2D **40**
Badsey Flds. La. WR11: Bad 2C **40**
Badsey La. WR11: Bad, Eves 1F **39**
(not continuous)
WR12: Will 1H **41**
Badsey Rd. WR11: Ald, Bad, Eves 1G **39**
Baffin Rd. WR2: Worc 3D **20**
Bagehott Cl. WR9: D Spa 3C **10**
Bagehott Rd. WR9: D Spa 3C **10**
Bagshaw Ct. WR10: Per 4D **34**
Bainbrigge Av. WR9: D Spa 1E **11**
Bakers Arc. WR10: Per 5D **34**
Bala Way WR5: Worc 3A **22**
Baldenhall WR14: Mal 1H **29**
Baldock Rd. WR14: Mal 2E **29**
Ballard Cl. HR8: Led 1B **42**
WR13: C Sto 1B **30**
Ballards Dr. WR13: Upp C 1D **30**
Balliol Rd. WR4: Worc 4A **18**
Balmoral Cl. WR3: Fern H 1C **14**
WR11: Eves 5E **37**
WR14: Mal 1G **27**
Bamburgh Cres. WR4: Warn 1E **19**
Bank Cres. HR8: Led 3C **42**
Bankside Cl. WR3: Worc 6E **13**
Bankside Ind. Est. HR8: Led 4A **42**
Banks Rd. WR11: Bad 1C **40**
Bank St. WR1: Worc 4D **4** (5F **17**)
WR14: Mal 5D **26**
Bannut Hill WR5: Kemp 6H **25**
Baradene La. WR2: R'ick 1A **20**
Barass Av. WR4: Warn 2E **19**
Barbel Cres. WR5: Worc 4G **21**
Barbers Cl. WR4: Worc 6B **14**
BARBOURNE 6F **13**
Barbourne Ct. *WR1: Worc* *2E 17*
(off Barbourne Cres.)
Barbourne Cres. WR1: Worc 2E **17**
Barbourne La. WR1: Worc 2E **17**
Barbourne Rd. WR1: Worc 2F **17**
Barbourne Ter. WR1: Worc 2E **17**
Barbourne Wlk. WR1: Worc 2E **17**
Barbourne Works WR3: Worc 6E **13**
Barker St. WR3: Worc 2H **17**
Barley Cres. WR4: Warn 1D **18**
Barley Orchard Ct. WR11: Eves 2E **39**
Barlows Bldg. WR2: Worc 5A **4**
Barnards Cl. WR11: Eves 3E **39**
WR14: Mal 2G **29**
BARNARD'S GREEN 1F **29**
Barnard's Grn. Rd. WR14: Mal 1E **29**
Barn Cl. WR2: Worc 1C **20**
Barneshall Av. WR5: Worc 3G **21**
Barnes Pl. WR5: Worc 3H **21**
Barnes Way WR5: Worc 3H **21**
Barnett Av. HR8: Led 3A **42**
Barnetts Cl. HR8: Led 3A **42**
Barns Cft. Way WR9: D Spa 2A **10**
Barrett Ri. WR14: Mal 5E **27**
Barry St. WR1: Worc 1E **5** (3G **17**)
Basepoint Bus. Cen.
WR11: Eves 5F **39**
Basin Rd. WR5: Worc 1F **21**
Basson Ct. WR11: Hamp 2B **38**
Bath Rd. WR5: Kemp 1G **25**
WR5: Worc 6E **5** (1G **21**)
(not continuous)
Batsford Rd. WR5: Worc 4A **22**
Battenhall Av. WR5: Worc 1H **21**
Batten Hall Lodge WR5: Worc 1H **21**

44 A-Z Worcester

Battenhall M. *WR5: Worc* 6A **18**
(off Sebright Av.)
Battenhall Pl. WR5: Worc 6G **5** (6H **17**)
Battenhall Ri. WR5: Worc 2A **22**
Battenhall Rd. WR5: Worc 6H **17**
Battenhall Wlk. WR5: Worc 6H **17**
Battisto Wlk. WR14: Mal 6G **27**
Battle Rd. WR5: Worc 1H **21**
Battleton Rd. WR11: Eves 3D **38**
BAUGHTON 1H **33**
Baveney Rd. WR2: Worc 1C **16**
Bawdsey Av. WR14: Mal 5F **27**
Baxters Wlk. WR14: Mal 6G **27**
Bayly Cl. WR11: Eves 3E **39**
Baynham Dr. WR5: Worc 1C **22**
Bays Mdw. WR9: D Spa 5D **8**
Beach Cl. WR11: Eves 2E **39**
Beaconhill Dr. WR2: Worc 1C **16**
Beacon Ho. WR14: Mal 4D **26**
Beacon Rd. WR14: W Mal 5B **28**
Bearcroft Av. WR4: Warn 1D **18**
Beauchamp Bus. Cen. WR14: Mal 3G **27**
Beauchamp La. WR2: C End 3D **24**
Beauchamp Rd. WR14: Mal 3D **26**
(not continuous)
Beaver Cl. WR2: Worc 3C **20**
Beckett Cl. WR3: Worc 5F **13**
Beckett Dr. WR3: Worc 5F **13**
Beckett Rd. WR3: Worc 5E **13**
Bedford Cl. WR10: Per 4C **34**
Bedwardine Cl. WR2: R'ick 1A **20**
Bedwardine Ho. WR2: Worc 4A **4** (5E **17**)
Bedwardine Rd. WR2: Worc 6D **16**
Beech Av. WR3: Worc 6F **13**
Beech Av. Nth. WR3: Worc 6G **13**
Beech Cl. WR14: Mal 2F **27**
Beechcombe Cl. WR10: Per 3D **34**
Beeches, The WR8: Rya 3D **32**
Beehive Pl. WR4: Warn 2E **19**
Beeston Gdns. WR4: Warn 1E **19**
Beggars Ash HR8: W'ton H 1B **42**
Begonia Cl. WR5: Worc 5G **21**
Belfry Rd. WR9: D Spa 3D **10**
Bellars Cl. WR14: Mal 1G **29**
Bellars Gdns. WR14: Mal 1H **29**
Bellar's La. WR14: Mal 1G **29**
Bell Cl. WR2: Hall 4C **12**
Belle Orchard HR8: Led 2B **42**
Belle Orchard Cl. HR8: Led 3B **42**
Belle Vue Ter. WR14: Mal 1D **28**
Bell Sq. WR1: Worc 4D **4**
Bell Tower
Evesham 1D **38**
Bell Yd. WR12: B'way 5G **41**
Belmont Lodge WR3: Worc 2H **17**
Belmont Rd. WR14: Mal 3C **26**
Belmont St. WR3: Worc 2H **17**
Belmont Wlk. WR3: Worc 1F **17**
Belvoir Bank WR14: Mal 4B **26**
Benbow Cl. WR14: Mal W 1E **31**
BENGEWORTH 2G **39**
Bentham Av. WR4: Warn 4E **19**
Benton Cl. WR14: Mal W 5F **31**
Berkeley Bus. Pk. WR4: Warn 6F **15**
Berkeley Cl. WR14: Whitt 2E **23**
Berkeley Ct. WR1: Worc 3D **4**
WR4: Warn .6D **14**
Berkeley Ho. *WR1: Worc* 4E **5**
(off New St.)
Berkeley St. WR1: Worc 2E **17**
Berkeley Way WR4: Warn 6D **14**
(not continuous)
Berkley Gdns. WR3: Fern H 3B **14**
Berrill Cl. WR9: D Spa 2F **11**
Berrow Ct. WR8: Upt Sev 4C **32**
Berry Cl. WR2: Pow 1A **24**
Berryfield Rd. WR11: Hamp 2A **38**
BERRY HILL 3C **8**
Berry Hill WR9: D Spa 4C **8**
Berry Hill Ind. Est. WR9: D Spa 3C **8**
Berwick St. WR5: Worc 2G **21**
Bestmans La. WR5: Kemp 6G **25**
Bethell Ct. HR8: Led 4B **42**
Betjeman Cl. WR10: Per 5D **34**
Betony Rd. WR14: Mal 3G **27**
BEVERE 2E **13**
Bevere Cl. WR3: Worc 4E **13**
Bevere Cl. Sth. WR3: Worc 4E **13**
Bevere Ct. WR3: Bev 3D **12**
Bevere Dr. WR3: Bev 4E **13**
Bevere Gallery 2E **13**
Bevere Grn. WR3: Bev 2E **13**
Bevere Ho. WR3: Bev 2E **13**
Bevere La. WR3: Bev 2E **13**

Beverley Way WR14: Mal 1C **26**
Bevington Ct. *WR5: Worc* 1F **21**
(off Layland Wlk.)
Bewdley Ct. *WR11: Eves* 1D **38**
(off Bewdley St.)
Bewdley La. WR11: Eves 1C **38**
Bewdley St. WR11: Eves 1C **38**
Bibsworth Av. WR12: B'way 5H **41**
Bibsworth La. WR12: B'way 5H **41**
(High St.)
WR12: B'way 3H **41**
(Leamington Rd.)
Bicton Av. WR5: Worc 3A **22**
Biddulph Way HR8: Led 5B **42**
Biggin Hill Cl. WR14: Mal 2C **26**
Bilford Av. WR3: Worc 6H **13**
Bilford Ct. WR3: Worc 6A **14**
Bilford Rd. WR3: Worc 6G **13**
Binyon Cl. WR11: Dad 3C **40**
Birchanger Grn. WR4: Warn 2E **19**
Birch Av. WR4: Worc 3A **18**
WR11: Eves .3F **39**
Birch Cl. HR8: Led 4B **42**
Birch Coppice WR9: D Spa 3D **10**
Birchfield Cl. WR3: Worc 2G **17**
Birchtree Gro. WR10: Per 3D **34**
Birchwood Rd. WR14: Worc 1C **26**
Birdlip Cl. WR4: Warn 1C **18**
Birlingham Cl. WR10: Per 6C **34**
Birmingham Rd. WR11: Bad 1C **40**
Birties of Worcester (Gallery) 5E **5** (5G **17**)
Bishops Av. WR3: Worc 2G **17**
Bishops Ct. WR13: C Sto 3A **30**
Bisley Cl. WR4: Warn 6C **14**
Bittern Rd. WR5: Worc 4H **21**
Blackberry Way WR11: Eves 5D **38**
Blackfriars Av. WR3: Worc 1C **10**
Blackfriars Ct. WR9: D Spa 6D **8**
Blackheath Way WR14: W Mal 1A **28**
Blackhill WR14: Mal W 4F **31**
Black Horse Wlk. WR1: Worc 3E **5** (4G **17**)
BLACKMORE PARK 5H **29**
Blackmore Pk. Ind. Est.
WR8: Han S .5H **29**
Blackmore Pk. Rd. WR13: Well 5F **29**
WR14: Mal W 5F **29**
Blackmore Rd. WR14: Mal 4C **26**
BLACKPOLE 6A **14**
Blackpole East WR3: Worc 5B **14**
Blackpole Retail Pk. WR3: Worc 6A **14**
Blackpole Rd. WR3: Worc 1A **18**
WR4: Worc .1A **18**
Blackpole Trad. Est. E. WR3: Worc 4B **14**
Blackpole Trad. Est. W. WR3: Hind 4A **14**
Blackthorn Cl. WR11: Eves 3G **39**
Blackthorne Cl. WR9: D Spa 3E **11**
Blackthorn Rd. WR4: Warn 1A **18**
Blagdon Cl. WR5: Worc 3B **22**
Blair Cl. WR4: Warn 1D **18**
Blake Av. WR9: D Spa 2B **10**
Blakefield Gdns. WR2: Worc 6A **4** (6D **16**)
Blakefield Rd. WR2: Worc 6D **16**
Blakefield Wlk. WR2: Worc 6D **16**
Blakeney Cl. WR9: D Spa 3E **11**
Blake St. WR5: Worc 3H **21**
Blandford Cl. WR13: Well 3G **31**
Blanquettes Av. WR3: Worc 1F **17**
Blanquettes St. WR3: Worc 1F **17**
Blayneys La. WR11: Eves 3D **36**
Blenheim Dr. HR8: Led 5C **42**
Blenheim Rd. WR2: Worc 4C **16**
Blind La. WR11: Eves 1C **38**
Blockhouse Cl. WR1: Worc 5F **5** (5G **17**)
Bloomfield Rd. WR2: Worc 1D **20**
Blossom Cl. WR5: Worc 4D **18**
Blossomfield Cl. WR11: Hamp 3B **38**
Bloxham Rd. WR12: B'way 4G **41**
Bluebell Cl. WR14: Mal 2G **29**
Bluebell Way WR11: Eves 5D **38**
Boat La. WR11: Eves 1C **38**
WR11: Off .3G **37**
Bodiam Cl. WR4: Warn 1E **19**
Bolston Rd. WR5: Worc 1C **21**
Bolton Av. WR4: Warn 2F **19**
Bomford Hill WR4: Warn 3D **18**
Bond Ind. Est. WR11: W'ford 6B **40**
Bond St. WR14: Mal 3E **27**
(not continuous)
Born Ct. HR8: Led 3C **42**
Borrowdale Dr. WR4: Warn 2C **18**
(not continuous)
Borrowdale Rd. WR14: Mal 1G **29**
Bosbury Rd. WR14: Mal 2D **26**
Boscobel Pl. WR1: Worc 3F **5** (4G **17**)
Boswell Ct. WR14: Mal 3E **27**

Boughton Av. WR2: Worc 6C **16**
Boughton Cl. WR2: Worc 6C **16**
Boughton Pk. Cl. WR2: Worc 1C **20**
Boughton St. WR2: Worc 6D **16**
Bourne Cl. WR9: D Spa 6D **8**
Bourne St. WR2: Worc 1F **17**
Bowden Grn. WR9: D Spa 3D **10**
Bower Hill WR9: D Spa 3D **10**
Bowhill WR2: C End 4D **24**
Bowl Extreme .6G **13**
BOWLING GREEN .6A **20**
Bowling Grn. WR8: Han C 1A **32**
Bowling Grn. Rd. WR2: Pow 6A **20**
Bowness Dr. WR4: Warn 2C **18**
Bowood La. WR5: Worc 2C **22**
Bozward St. WR2: Worc 5D **16**
Bracken Cl. WR3: Worc 3C **16**
Bracken Way WR14: Mal 2G **27**
Bradford Pl. WR5: Worc 6C **18**
Bradley Ct. WR5: Worc 1F **21**
Bradley Dr. WR14: Mal 2C **26**
BRADLOW 1D **42**
Bramble Cl. WR14: Mal 4G **27**
Bramble Gdns. WR5: Worc 4D **18**
Bramhope Cl. WR4: Warn 3C **18**
Bramley Av. WR2: Worc 1C **16**
Bramley Cl. HR8: Led 5B **42**
WR2: Pow 6A **20**
Bramley Dr. WR11: Eves 5E **39**
Bramley Pl. WR2: Worc 1C **16**
BRAND GREEN 4C **30**
Bransford Rd. WR2: R'ick, Worc . . .6A **4** (1A **20**)
Brantwood Cl. WR4: Warn 2C **18**
Brantwood Cl. WR9: D Spa 2E **11**
Brantwood Rd. WR9: D Spa 2E **11**
Bray Av. HR8: Led 4C **42**
Braymoor Rd. WR1: Worc 1C **4** (3F **17**)
BRAYSWICK 3A **24**
Bream Cl. WR5: Worc 4G **21**
Brecon Av. WR4: Warn 1F **19**
Brecon Cl. WR9: D Spa 2A **10**
Bredon Cl. WR12: B'way 5F **41**
Bredon Gro. WR14: Mal 3G **29**
Bredon Hill Vw. WR11: Hamp 2A **38**
Bredon Vw. WR12: B'way 5H **41**
Brentwood Cl. WR5: Worc 6B **18**
Bretforton Rd. WR11: Bad 1C **40**
Brewers La. WR11: Bad 2C **40**
Brewery Wlk. WR1: Worc 3F **17**
Briar Cl. WR11: Eves 5D **36**
Briar Cl. Bus. Pk. WR11: Eves 5C **36**
BRIAR HILL 1A **10**
Briar Mill WR9: D Spa 6B **8**
BRICKFIELDS 1B **18**
Brickfields Rd. WR4: Worc 1A **18**
Brickfields Wlk. WR3: Worc 1A **18**
Brick Kiln St. WR11: Eves 1D **38**
Bridgemans Cl. WR12: B'way 4H **41**
Bridge St. HR8: Led 3A **42**
WR1: Worc 4C **4** (5F **17**)
WR10: Per .5E **35**
WR11: Eves .1D **38**
Bridgnorth Row WR4: Warn 6E **15**
Bridgwater Rd. WR4: Warn 6F **15**
Bright Av. WR4: Warn 3E **19**
Brimstone Cl. WR5: Worc 4A **22**
Brindley Cl. WR4: Warn 6D **14**
Brindley Rd. WR4: Warn 6D **14**
Brine Pits La. WR9: Wych 1G **9**
Britannia Rd. WR1: Worc 1C **4** (3F **17**)
BRITANNIA SQUARE 1C **4** (3F **17**)
Britannia Sq. WR1: Worc 1B **4** (3F **17**)
Britannia Way WR14: Mal 3G **27**
British Camp Rd. WR13: C Sto 6A **30**
Britten Dr. WR14: Mal 3F **29**
Broad Down Cl. WR14: Mal 2C **26**
Broadfield Cres. WR3: Fern H 2B **14**
Broadfield Gdns. WR4: Warn 1D **18**
Broadheath Cl. WR9: D Spa 3C **10**
Broadheath La. WR2: Hall 5A **12**
Broadlands Dr. WR14: Mal 3B **26**
Broadmeadow WR9: D Spa 1B **10**
Broads Bank WR14: Mal 6D **26**
Broad St. WR1: Worc 4D **4** (5F **17**)
WR10: Per .5D **34**
BROADWAY 5G **41**
Broadway Caravan Club Site
WR12: B'way 4E **41**
Broadway Gravel Pit Nature Reserve 5E **41**
Broadway Gro. WR2: Worc 6B **16**
Broadway Rd. WR11: Eves, W'ford 2F **39**
WR12: Will .2H **41**
Broadwood Dr. WR13: C Sto 1C **30**
Broadwood Pk. WR13: C Sto 1C **30**

Brockhampton Cl. WR4: Warn 6B 14
Brockhill La. WR5: B Vill 4B 22
Brockhill Rd. WR13: C Sto 6A 28
   WR14: W Mal 4A 28
BROCKHILL VILLAGE 5B 22
Brock La. WR14: Mal 2C 26
Brockweir WR3: Worc 1H 17
Bromley Cl. WR8: Upt Sev 5A 32
Bromsgrove Rd.
   WR9: D Spa, Elm, Rash 6E 9
Bromsgrove St. WR3: Worc 1F 17
Bromwich La. WR2: Worc 6A 4 (6E 17)
Bromwich Pde. WR2: Worc 6D 4 (1F 21)
Bromwich Rd. WR2: Worc 6B 4 (3E 21)
Bromyard Rd. HR8: Led 1B 42
   WR2: Worc 6A 4 (5A 16)
Bromyard Rd. Ind. Est. HR8: Led 1B 42
Bromyard Ter. WR2: Worc 5A 4 (5E 17)
Bronsil Cl. WR5: Worc 1C 22
Bronsil Dr. WR14: Mal 1D 26
Bronte Dr. HR8: Led 3A 42
Brook Cl. WR5: Kemp 3H 25
BROOK END 3H 25
Brookend La. WR5: Kemp 3G 25
Brooke Rd. HR8: Led 2A 42
Brook Farm Dr. WR14: Mal 3G 29
Brookfield WR14: Mal 2F 27
Brookmill Cl. WR13: C Sto 3H 29
Brookside WR5: Kemp 3G 25
   WR11: Hamp 3B 38
   WR13: C Sto 2A 30
   WR13: Well 3G 31
   WR14: Mal 2G 27
Brookside Rd. WR2: Worc 4B 16
Brook St. WR1: Worc 2F 17
Brookthorpe Cl. WR4: Warn 6C 14
Brook Way WR10: W Pid 1G 35
Broomhall Cotts. WR5: Kemp 6B 22
Broomhall Grn. WR5: Worc 4A 22
Broomhall La. WR5: Kemp 1G 25
Broomhall Way WR5: Worc 5G 21
Broom Mdw. WR3: Fern H 2B 14
Brownes Way WR2: Hall 3B 12
Brown Heath La. WR3: M Hus 2F 15
   WR9: New 2F 15
Browning Cl. WR3: Worc 6G 13
Browning Ct. WR14: Mal 5E 27
Browning Rd. HR8: Led 3A 42
Brown Sq. WR8: Upt Sev 3C 32
Brown St. WR2: Worc 1E 21
Brunswick Cl. WR2: Worc 3D 20
Bryony Cl. WR14: Mal 1E 26
Buckholt Bus. Cen. WR4: Warn 5C 14
Buckholt Dr. WR4: Warn 5B 14
Buckingham Cl. WR14: Mal 1G 27
Buck St. WR2: Worc 5D 16
Bullfinch Cl. WR5: Worc 4H 21
Bull Ring WR2: Worc 5A 4 (5E 17)
Bunns Rd. WR5: Worc 3H 21
Burdett Pl. WR4: Warn 3E 19
Burford Cl. WR4: Warn 6C 14
Burford Gdns. WR11: Eves 1E 39
Burford Rd. WR11: Eves 1E 39
Burgess Cl. WR4: Warn 4E 19
Burleigh Rd. WR2: Worc 4B 16
Burlingham Av. WR11: Eves 1F 39
Burlingham Ct. WR11: Eves 6D 36
   (off Briar Cl.)
Burma Cl. WR11: Eves 2E 39
Burnham Cl. WR5: Worc 3H 21
Burnsall Cl. WR4: Warn 3C 18
Durrish St. WR9: D Spa 6D 8
   (not continuous)
Burrows Cl. WR14: Mal 6G 27
Burtree Av. WR4: Warn 2E 19
BURY END 6D 32
Buryend WR8: Upt Sev 6D 32
Buryfields Wlk. WR8: Upt Sev 4C 32
Bush La. WR2: C End 4B 24
Bush Wlk. WR2: Worc 5A 4 (5E 17)
Butcher Row House Folk Mus. 3C 42
   (off Church La.)
Butcher's Wlk. WR3: Fern H 2C 14
Buttercup Cl. WR11: Eves 1G 39
Buttercup Wlk. WR14: Mal 2C 26
Butterfly Cres. WR11: Eves 2F 39
Buttermere Dr. WR4: Warn 1C 18
Butts, The WR1: Worc 3C 4 (4F 17)
   WR9: D Spa 1B 10
Butts Pde. WR1: Worc 3B 4 (4E 17)
Byefields WR5: Kemp 5G 25
Bye Rd. WR14: Mal 2G 29
Bye St. HR8: Led 3B 42
Byfield Ri. WR5: Worc 3G 5 (4H 17)

Byron Cl. WR2: Pow 1A 24
   WR14: Mal 5E 27

C

Cabbage La. HR8: Led 3C 42
Caister Av. WR4: Warn 1E 19
Calder Cl. WR9: D Spa 2B 10
Calder Rd. WR5: Worc 4A 18
Caldy Av. WR5: Worc 3A 22
Cales Av. WR14: Mal 3C 26
Calgary Dr. WR2: Worc 2D 20
CALLOW END 4D 24
Callow End HR8: Led 1B 42
Camberwell Dr. WR5: Worc 4A 22
Cambrai Dr. WR5: B Vill 5B 22
   (not continuous)
Cambria Rd. WR11: Eves 6D 36
Cambridge Cl. WR14: Mal W 5F 31
Camden Pl. WR1: Worc 1D 4 (3F 17)
Cameron Ct. WR14: Mal 3E 29
Camp Furlong WR9: D Spa 2B 10
Camp Hill WR9: D Spa 2B 10
   (off Bower Hill)
   WR14: W Mal 6A 26
Camp Hill Av. WR5: Worc 1H 21
Camp Hill Rd. WR5: Worc 6H 17
Campion Dr. WR14: Mal 2H 29
Camp La. WR2: Grim 2C 12
Canada Way WR2: Worc 2D 20
Canal Side WR3: Worc 1G 17
Canalside Office Complex WR1: Worc 2F 5
Canal Wlk. HR8: Led 4B 42
Cangle La. WR4: Warn 2E 19
Cannon St. WR5: Worc 1A 22
Canterbury Rd. WR5: Worc 5B 18
Captain's La. WR9: Odd 5G 11
Carden Cl. WR1: Worc 5F 5 (5G 17)
Carden St. WR1: Worc 5E 5 (5G 17)
Carisbrooke Av. WR4: Warn 1E 19
Carlisle Rd. WR5: Worc 5C 18
Carlton Rd. WR14: Mal 4D 26
Carnforth Dr. WR4: Warn 1B 18
Carp WR5: Worc 4G 21
Carriage Cl. WR2: Worc 4D 16
Carrock Fell WR4: Warn 2C 18
Carters Cl. WR4: Worc 3B 18
Cartmel Cl. WR4: Warn 1D 18
Cartwright Av. WR4: Warn 4E 19
Castell Pl. WR4: Warn 6E 15
Castle Cl. WR3: Worc 5F 13
Castle Pl. WR1: Worc 6E 5 (6G 17)
Castle St. WR1: Worc 2C 4 (4F 17)
   WR11: Eves 1E 39
Catalpa Cl. WR14: Mal 1D 26
Catherine Rd. WR2: Worc 1C 20
Catbrook WR3: Worc 1C 16
Causeway La. WR8: Upt Sev 4C 32
Cavendish St. WR9: Worc 2G 21
Caversham Ct. WR3: Worc 1G 5 (3H 17)
Cecilia Av. WR2: Worc 1C 16
Cecilia Pl. WR2: Worc 1C 16
Cecil Rd. WR5: Worc 4G 5 (5H 17)
Cedar Av. WR4: Warn 1A 18
   WR14: Mal 4F 27
Cedar Cl. WR9: D Spa 3D 10
Cedar Ct. HR8: Led 3C 42
Cedars, The WR3: Fern H 2C 14
   WR5: Worc 1A 22
   WR14: Mal 3D 26
Cedarwood Gdns. WR11: Eves 2F 39
Celandine Dr. WR5: Worc 5H 21
Celandine Way WR11: Eves 5C 38
Celvestune Way WR9: D Spa 2B 10
Central Pk. WR5: Worc 5H 5 (5H 17)
Chacewater Av. WR3: Worc 6E 13
Chacewater Cres. WR3: Worc 6E 13
CHADBURY 1A 36
Chadbury Rd. WR11: Chad, Len 2A 36
Chadwick WR4: Warn 3E 19
Chalfont Cl. WR3: Worc 6F 13
Chalford Dr. WR4: Warn 6C 14
Challenger Cl. HR8: Led 1B 42
   WR14: Mal 6F 27
Chalverton Ct. WR9: D Spa 2A 10
Chamberlain Rd. WR2: Worc 2D 20
Chance La. WR14: Mal 6H 27
Chances Pitch WR13: C Sto 5G 29
Chantry Ho. WR2: Worc 5A 4 (5D 16)
Chapel Ct. WR5: Worc 5F 5
Chapel La. WR9: Omb 5A 6
   WR10: W Pid 2H 35
   WR11: Ald 1A 40

Chapel M. WR9: Wych 2E 9
   (not continuous)
Chapel Rd. WR5: Kemp 4G 25
Chapel St. WR11: Bad 2C 40
   WR11: Eves 1D 38
Chapel Wlk. WR1: Worc 4D 4
Chapter Meadows 6C 4 (6F 17)
Charity Cres. WR11: Eves 4D 38
Charland Ct. WR9: D Spa 4B 8
Charlecot Rd. WR9: D Spa 2E 11
Charlemont WR5: B Vill 5B 22
Charles Cl. WR11: Eves 2D 38
Charles Dickens Cl. WR9: D Spa 3C 10
Charles Hastings Way
   WR5: Worc 5D 18
Charles Henry Rd. WR9: D Spa 6E 9
Charles Orchard WR8: Upt Sev 5C 32
Charles St. WR1: Worc 4E 5 (5G 17)
   (not continuous)
Charles Way WR14: Mal 4F 27
Charlock Rd. WR14: Mal 2H 29
Charlotte Bronte Dr. WR9: D Spa 3C 10
Charlton Cl. WR11: Hamp 1A 38
Charnwood Cl. WR5: Worc 2D 20
Charter Pl. WR1: Worc 2C 4 (4F 17)
Chase End Cl. WR5: Worc 2C 22
   WR14: Mal 2C 26
Chase M. WR10: Per 5D 34
   (off Head St.)
Chase Rd. WR13: Upp C 6B 28
   WR14: Mal W 4F 31
Chatcombe Dr. WR4: Warn 6C 14
CHAWSON 2B 10
Chawson La. WR9: D Spa, Salw 3A 10
Chawson Pleck WR9: D Spa 1B 10
Chawson Rd. WR9: D Spa 1C 10
CHAWSON VALLEY 2A 10
Checketts Cl. WR3: Worc 6F 13
   WR10: Pin 1A 34
Checketts Cl. WR3: Worc 5F 13
Checketts La. WR3: Worc 5F 13
Checketts La. Ind. Est.
   WR3: Worc 5F 13
Chedworth Cl. WR4: Warn 6C 14
Chedworth Dr. WR4: Warn 6C 14
Chelmsford Ct. WR5: Worc 6B 18
Chelmsford Dr. WR5: Worc 6B 18
Cheltenham Rd. WR11: Eves, Hint G 6C 38
   WR12: B'way 6E 41
Chepstow Av. WR4: Warn 1D 18
Chequers Ct. WR14: Mal 3G 27
Chequers La. WR2: Worc 4A 4 (5E 17)
   WR9: Wych 2E 9
Cherington Cl. WR4: Warn 6B 14
Cherry Cl. WR9: D Spa 2F 11
   WR11: Eves 3F 39
   WR11: Off 2G 37
CHERRY ORCHARD 2G 21
Cherry Orchard WR8: Upt Sev 4C 32
   WR10: Per 4D 34
Cherry Orchard Ho. WR10: Per 3D 34
Cherry St. WR5: Worc 1G 21
Cherry Tree Dr. WR14: Mal W 5D 28
Cherry Tree Wlk. WR1: Worc 3D 4 (4F 17)
Cherwell Cl. WR4: Warn 3B 18
Cherwell Rd. WR4: Warn 3B 18
Cheshire Cheese Entry WR1: Worc 2D 4
Chester Cl. WR5: Worc 6B 18
Chester Pl. WR5: Mal 3C 26
Chesterton Gdns. WR5: Worc 4C 18
Chestnut Cl. HR8: Led 1D 42
   WR3: Fern H 2B 14
   WR11: Ald 1A 40
   WR11: Hamp 3B 38
   WR13: Well 3G 31
Chestnut Ct. WR14: Mal 1F 29
Chestnut Dr. WR14: Mal W 5D 28
Chestnut La. WR1: Worc 1E 5 (3G 17)
Chestnut Spinney WR9: D Spa 3D 10
Chestnut St. WR1: Worc 1D 4 (3F 17)
Chestnut Wlk. WR1: Worc 1D 4 (3F 17)
   WR9: Omb 4A 6
Chevenham Cl. WR13: C Sto 2A 30
Cheviot Cl. WR4: Warn 3B 18
Childer Rd. HR8: Led 4A 42
Childswickham Rd. WR12: B'way 5E 41
Chilham Pl. WR14: Mal 1E 19
Chiltern Cl. WR4: Warn 3B 18
Chorley Rd. WR9: D Spa 6D 8
Christ Church Rd. WR14: Mal 1E 29
Christchurch Rd. WR4: Worc 4A 18
   WR14: Mal 3E 29
Christina Cl. WR5: Kemp 4G 25
Christine Av. WR2: R'ick 2A 20
Chub Cl. WR5: Worc 4G 21

Church Cl. WR2: Worc 6A **4** (6D **16**)
  WR12: B'way 6F **41**
Churchdown Rd. WR14: Mal 3F **29**
CHURCH END 1A **32**
Church End WR11: Bad 2C **40**
Church Farm WR10: W Pid 2G **35**
Churchill Av. WR9: D Spa 2C **10**
Churchill Ct. WR11: Hamp 2B **38**
Churchill Dr. WR14: Mal 1F **27**
Churchill Mdw. HR8: Led 4A **42**
Church La. HR8: Led 3C **42**
  WR2: Hall 4B **12**
  WR3: M Hus 1D **14**
  WR5: Nort 5C **22**
  WR5: Whitt 3D **22**
  WR8: E Cro 1F **33**
  WR9: Omb .6A **6**
  WR9: Tib 6H **15**
  WR9: Wych 1E **9**
  WR10: Pin 2B **34**
Church Mdw. Ct. WR14: Mal 5D **26**
Church Rd. HR8: Led 3C **42**
  WR3: Worc 1D **14**
  WR9: D Spa 5E **9**
  WR11: Hamp 3B **38**
  WR14: Mal 3E **27**
Church Row WR10: Per 5D **34**
Church St. HR8: Led 3C **42**
  WR1: Worc 4E **5** (5G **17**)
  WR5: Kemp 4F **25**
  WR8: Upt Sev 3C **32**
  WR10: Per 5D **34**
  WR11: Eves 2E **39**
  WR11: Off 2G **37**
  WR12: B'way 6F **41**
  WR12: Will 1H **41**
  WR14: Mal 1D **28**
Church Ter. WR2: Worc 6A **4** (6D **16**)
  WR5: Whitt 3D **22**
Church Wlk. WR2: Worc 5A **4** (5E **17**)
  WR8: Upt Sev 4C **32**
  WR10: Per 5D **34**
  WR14: Mal 6D **26**
Cirencester Pl. WR14: Warn 6D **14**
City Arc. WR1: Worc 4E **5**
City Art Gallery & Mus. 2D **4** (4F **17**)
City Wall 4E **5**
City Walls Rd. WR1: Worc . . .3E **5** (4G **17**)
CLAINES 3G **13**
Claines La. WR3: Clain 2F **13**
Claphill La. WR2: R'ick 6A **16**
Claremont Ct. WR14: Mal W 2E **31**
Clarence Av. WR14: Mal 2E **31**
Clarence Rd. WR14: Mal 1D **28**
Clare Rd. WR14: Mal 6F **27**
Clare St. WR1: Worc 5E **5** (5G **17**)
Clare Wlk. WR14: Mal 5C **26**
Clarks Hill Ri. WR11: Hamp 2B **38**
Clarkson Gdns. WR4: Warn 3E **19**
Claverham Cl. WR2: Worc 1E **21**
Clayfield Dr. WR14: Mal 3C **26**
Clayhall Rd. WR9: D Spa 2E **11**
Cleeve Dr. WR4: Warn 1C **18**
Clee Vw. WR9: D Spa 1C **10**
Clementi Ct. WR11: Eves 1F **39**
Clerkenwell Cres. WR14: Mal 5E **27**
Clifford Cl. WR9: D Spa 4C **10**
Clifford Rd. WR9: D Spa 4C **10**
Close, The WR10: W Pid 1H **35**
  WR11: Eves 1E **39**
Clover Way WR14: Mal 3G **29**
Clyde Av. WR11: Eves 2F **39**
Clydesdale Cl. WR9: D Spa 3F **11**
Clydesdale Ri. WR9: D Spa 3F **11**
Clydesdale Rd. WR9: D Spa 3F **11**
Coach Ho. Lodge WR1: Worc 5D **4**
Coachman's Ct. HR8: Led 4A **42**
               (off Lit. Marcle Rd.)
Cobden Av. WR4: Warn 3E **19**
Coberley Cl. WR14: Mal 1C **28**
Cobham Cl. WR13: Woll 3G **31**
Cobham Ct. WR9: D Spa 1D **10**
Cobham Rd. WR10: Per 1E **35**
Cockshot Rd. WR14: Mal 4D **26**
                (not continuous)
Cockshute Hill WR9: D Spa 1F **11**
Coldicott Gdns. WR11: Eves 4F **39**
Cole Hill WR5: Worc 5F **5** (6H **17**)
Colehurst Pk. WR5: Worc 1G **5**
Coleridge Cl. WR3: Worc 1G **17**
Coleridge Ct. WR14: Mal 5E **27**
Colesborne Cl. WR4: Warn 6B **14**
Coley Cl. WR3: Fern H 2C **14**
Colford Cl. WR9: D Spa 2A **10**

Colin Rd. WR3: Worc 5E **13**
College Grn. WR1: Worc 6D **4** (6F **17**)
College Gro. WR14: Mal 3D **28**
College M. WR14: Mal 2D **28**
College Precincts WR1: Worc 5E **5** (5G **17**)
College Rd. WR14: Mal 2D **28**
College St. WR1: Worc 5E **5** (5G **17**)
College Yd. WR1: Worc 5D **4** (5F **17**)
Colletts Flds. WR12: B'way 5H **41**
Colletts Gdns. WR12: B'way 5H **41**
COLLETTS GREEN 6A **20**
Colletts Grn. Rd. WR2: Pow 5A **20**
Collin Cl. WR12: Will 1H **41**
Collinghurst Ho. WR8: Upt Sev 3C **32**
Collings Av. WR4: Warn 4E **19**
Collin La. WR12: B'way 2E **41**
  WR12: Will 2G **41**
Collinsfield WR11: Eves 5D **36**
Colman Rd. WR9: D Spa 6D **8**
Coltishall Cl. WR5: Worc 3H **21**
Columbia Dr. WR2: Worc 2C **20**
Columbine Gro. WR11: Eves 4C **38**
COLWALL .1B **30**
COLWALL GREEN 4A **30**
Colwall Ho. *WR14: Mal* *2C **26***
               (off Hill Vw. Rd.)
Colwall Station (Rail) 2B **30**
Combined Court
  Worcester 2D **4** (4F **17**)
Comer Av. WR2: Worc 5D **16**
Comer Gdns. WR2: Worc 4C **16**
Comer Rd. WR2: Worc 4D **16**
Commandery St. WR5: Worc 5F **5**
Commandery Museum, The 6F **5** (6G **17**)
Commandery Rd. WR1: Worc 6E **5** (6G **17**)
Common Gdn. HR8: Led 3C **42**
Common Rd. WR11: Eves 6E **37**
Como Rd. WR14: Mal 6D **26**
Compton Rd. WR5: Worc 5H **5** (5H **17**)
Conduit Hill WR11: Eves 1E **39**
Conduit Ho. *WR11: Eves* *1E **39***
               (off Rynal Pl.)
Coney Grn. Cl. WR4: Warn 1D **18**
Conisborough WR4: Warn 1E **19**
Coniston Cl. WR4: Warn 2C **18**
  WR14: Mal 3G **29**
Connaught Cl. WR5: Worc 3H **21**
Conningsby Dr. WR10: Per 5B **34**
Constance Rd. WR3: Worc 5D **12**
Conway Dr. WR4: Warn 3B **18**
Conwy Dr. WR11: Eves 2F **39**
Cooks Hill WR10: Wick 6H **35**
Coombefield Rd. WR11: W'ford 6B **40**
Coombs Rd. WR3: Worc 6F **13**
Coopers Cl. WR4: Worc 1B **18**
Cooper's La. WR11: Eves 2E **39**
Cooper St. WR14: Mal 2C **26**
COPCUT 3B **10**
Copcut Ct. WR9: D Spa 2B **10**
Copcut Golf Cen. 4B **10**
Copcut La. WR9: Cop, Salw 3A **10**
Copenhagen St. WR1: Worc 5D **4** (5F **17**)
Cope Rd. WR3: Worc 6F **13**
Coppice Cl. WR2: Hall 2B **12**
  WR9: D Spa 4B **8**
  WR14: Mal 1C **26**
Coppice Way WR9: D Spa 4A **8**
Copsewood Av. WR5: Worc 4D **18**
Corbett Av. WR9: D Spa 2D **10**
Corbett St. WR9: D Spa 1D **10**
Corfe Av. WR4: Warn 1E **19**
Cormorant Ri. WR2: Worc 3E **21**
Cornflower Dr. WR11: Eves 5B **36**
Corn Mkt. WR1: Worc 4E **5** (5G **17**)
Cornmarket Ct. *WR1: Worc* *4E **5***
               (off Corn Mkt.)
Cornmeadow Grn. WR3: Worc 4F **13**
Cornmeadow La. WR3: Clain, Worc 5F **13**
Cornmill Rd. WR11: Eves 4C **38**
Cornmore WR10: Per 6B **34**
               (not continuous)
Coronation Av. WR2: R'ick 1A **20**
Coronation Rd. WR14: Mal 2F **27**
Coronation St. WR11: Eves 1F **39**
Corunna Cl. WR5: B Vill 5B **22**
Cosgrove Cl. WR3: Worc 5A **14**
Cotland WR3: Worc 2H **17**
Cotswold Cl. WR12: B'way 6G **41**
Cotswold Rd. WR14: Mal 6F **27**
Cotswold Vw. *WR11: Eves* *1D **38***
               (off Mill Bank)
Cotswold Way WR4: Warn 5B **14**
Cottage Row *WR8: Upt Sev* *3C **32***
               (off Gardens Wlk.)

County Court
  Evesham .6D **36**
Court, The WR12: B'way 5G **41**
Court Gdns. WR5: Kemp 4F **25**
  WR14: Mal 1F **29**
Court Gth. WR5: Kemp 4F **25**
Courtland Cl. WR3: Worc 4E **13**
Court La. WR11: Off 1G **37**
Court Lea WR8: Holl G 2E **33**
Court Mdw. WR5: Kemp 4F **25**
Court Rd. WR14: Mal 2E **29**
Court Row *WR8: Upt Sev* *4C **32***
               (off Oak St.)
Court St. WR8: Upt Sev 3C **32**
Cove Gdns. WR3: Worc 6E **13**
Coventry Av. WR2: Worc 2E **21**
Coventry Ter. WR10: Per 1D **34**
Covercroft WR9: D Spa 6D **8**
Cover Arm. WR4: Warn 3D **18**
Cow La. DY13: S'ton 1B **6**
  WR9: Dov .1B **6**
Cowl Barn La. WR13: C Sto 1B **30**
Cowleigh Bank WR14: Mal 4B **26**
COWLEIGH PARK 3A **26**
Cowleigh Rd. WR13: Crad 3A **26**
  WR14: Mal 3A **26**
Cowleys Way WR10: Per 4D **34**
Cowl St. WR11: Eves 1D **38**
Coxlea Cl. WR11: Eves 6C **36**
Coxwell Dr. WR14: Mal 4F **27**
Crab Apple Way WR11: Eves 5F **39**
Crane Dr. WR2: Worc 3E **21**
Cranesbill Dr. WR5: Worc 4H **21**
Cranham Dr. WR4: Warn 6C **14**
Cranham Est., The WR4: Warn 5B **14**
Crantham Cl. WR4: Warn 1C **18**
Craven Cl. WR11: Eves 1E **39**
Crescent, The WR13: C Sto 2A **30**
  WR14: Mal W 4F **31**
Crescent Rd. WR13: C Sto 2A **30**
Crescent Vs. WR3: Worc 1G **5**
Cresswell Cl. WR3: Fern H 3A **14**
Crickley Dr. WR4: Warn 6C **14**
Cripplegate Ho. WR2: Worc 5A **4**
Crispin Dr. WR14: Mal 1F **27**
Croft Bank WR14: W Mal 1A **26**
Croftdown Ct. WR14: Mal 1D **28**
Crofters Cl. WR9: D Spa 4B **8**
Crofters End WR9: D Spa 3B **8**
Crofters Grn. *WR9: D Spa* *3B **8***
               (off Crofters Way)
Crofters Hill WR9: D Spa 3B **8**
Crofters Way WR9: D Spa 4B **8**
Croft Farm Dr. WR4: W Mal 6A **26**
Croft Gdns. WR12: B'way 6G **41**
Croft Rd. WR1: Worc 4C **4** (4F **17**)
  WR11: Eves 5D **36**
Cromwell Ct. WR14: Mal 3E **27**
Cromwell Cres. WR5: Worc 1B **22**
Cromwell Cres. La. WR5: Worc 1A **22**
Cromwell Rd. WR2: Pow 1A **24**
  WR14: Mal 3E **27**
Cromwell St. WR1: Worc 3G **5** (4H **17**)
Crookbarrow Rd. WR5: B Vill 5B **22**
Crookbarrow Way WR5: Worc 4A **22**
Croome Rd. WR2: Worc 2D **20**
Cross, The WR1: Worc 3D **4** (4F **17**)
  WR10: W Pid 1G **35**
Crossley Rd. WR5: Worc 1F **21**
Crowngate Shop. Cen. WR1: Worc . . .4D **4** (5F **17**)
               (not continuous)
Crown Grn. Ct. WR11: Eves 1D **4**
Crown La. WR9: Wych 1E **9**
Crown Lea Av. WR14: Mal 1G **29**
Crownlea Ct. WR14: Mal 1G **29**
Crown Pas. WR1: Worc 3D **4** (4F **17**)
Crown St. WR3: Worc 1F **17**
Crown Wlk. WR1: Worc 1F **17**
Crucible Bus. Pk. WR5: Nort 6G **23**
Crumpton Hill WR13: Stor 1A **26**
Crumpton Hill Rd. WR13: Stor 1A **26**
Crutch La. WR9: D Spa 5E **9**
  WR9: Elm .3E **9**
Cumberland St. WR1: Worc 2F **17**
Cut Throat La. HR8: Brad 1D **42**
  WR8: Upt Sev 4A **32**
Cypress Cl. WR11: Eves 4F **39**
Cypress St. WR3: Worc 1F **17**
Cyril Rd. WR3: Worc 3H **17**

D

Dace Rd. WR5: Worc 4G **21**
Daisy Cl. WR11: Eves 1G **39**

Dalbury Cl. WR6: Mal 3D 26
Dale, The WR9: D Spa 1B 10
Dalegarth Ct. WR4: Warn 1D 18
   (off Martindale Cl.)
Damaskfield WR4: Warn 3E 19
Damson Dr. WR11: Hamp 2A 38
Dancox Ho. WR2: Worc 5A 4 (5E 17)
Danebury Pk. WR6: Mal 4B 26
Danes Cl. WR14: Mal 4F 27
Danes Grn. WR3: Clain 2G 13
Daniel Ho. WR11: Eves 5D 36
   (off St Christopher Ct.)
Danube Cl. WR9: D Spa 3B 10
Dark La. DY13: S'ton 1A 6
Dart Rd. WR5: Worc 4B 18
Darwin Av. WR5: Worc 4C 18
Darwin Cl. WR5: Kemp 5G 25
Daston Cl. WR12: B'way 5H 41
Daty Cft. WR4: Warn 3D 18
Davenham Cl. WR14: Mal 6E 27
Davies Rd. WR11: Eves 3D 38
Dawes Ct. HR8: Led 2B 42
DAWSHILL .5A 20
Dawson Cl. WR2: Worc 3D 20
Deacle Pl. WR11: Eves 1F 39
Deal Cres. WR4: Warn 1E 19
Deane Cl. WR2: Pow 1A 24
Deansway WR1: Worc 4D 4 (5F 17)
Debdale Av. WR4: Warn 2D 18
DEBLINS GREEN 4A 24
Deer Av. WR5: Worc 3B 22
Deerhurst Ter. WR10: Per 1D 34
Dee Way WR4: Warn 4B 18
Defford Rd. WR10: Per 6A 34
De La Bere Cl. WR11: Eves 6D 36
Delamere Rd. WR14: Mal 6F 27
Denison Cl. WR14: Mal 5F 27
Dent Cl. WR5: Worc 5F 5 (5G 17)
Derby Rd. WR5: Worc 6F 5 (6G 17)
Dereham Ct. WR14: Mal 4D 26
Derries, The WR3: Fern H 2C 14
Derwent Cl. WR4: Warn 1B 18
Derwent Gro. WR9: D Spa 2B 8
De Salis Ct. WR9: Hamp L 2B 8
De Salis Dr. WR9: Hamp L 2B 8
Devon Rd. WR5: Worc 6B 18
De Walden Rd. WR14: W Mal 6A 26
De Wyche Cl. WR9: Wych 2E 9
De Wyche Rd. WR9: Wych 2E 9
Dickinson Cl. WR3: Worc 6G 13
Digby Rd. WR11: Eves 2F 39
DIGLIS 1F 21
Diglis Av. WR1: Worc 6F 17
Diglis Ct. WR5: Worc 6G 17
   (off Diglis Rd.)
Diglis Dock Rd. WR5: Worc 2F 21
Diglis La. WR5: Worc 1G 21
Diglis Pde. WR1: Worc 6D 4 (6F 17)
   WR5: Worc 1F 21
Diglis Rd. WR5: Worc 1G 21
Dilmore Av. WR3: Fern H 2A 14
Dilmore La. WR3: Clain, Fern H 1A 14
Dinchall Rd. WR5: Worc 1C 22
DINES GREEN 5B 16
Dinmore Cl. WR5: Worc 4A 22
Dixey Cl. WR14: Mal 4C 26
Dockeray Av. WR4: Warn 2E 19
Dodderhill Rd. WR9: D Spa 5E 9
Dogwood Cl. WR14: Mal 4G 27
Dolday WR1: Worc 4C 4 (5F 17)
Dolphin Cl. WR2: Worc 3C 16
Donaldson Cl. WR1: Worc 6F 5
Donney Brook WR11: Eves 2F 39
Don Rd. WR4: Worc 4B 18
Dormouse Cft. WR5: Worc 3B 22
Doughty Ct. WR1: Worc 6E 5
Doultons Wharf WR5: Worc 4G 5
Dove Cl. WR4: Worc 4B 18
Dovecote Rd. WR9: D Spa 2E 11
Dover Av. WR4: Warn 1E 19
DOVERDALE 1D 6
Doverdale Cl. WR9: D Spa 1C 10
Doverdale La. WR9: Dov, Hamp L 1E 7
Doverdale Pk. Homes WR9: Hamp L 2B 8
Dowland Gdns. WR2: Worc 4B 16
Dowles Cft. WR9: D Spa 6C 8
Dragonfly Grn. WR5: Worc 3B 22
Drake Av. WR2: Worc 4B 16
Drake Pl. WR2: Worc 5B 16
Drakes Lea WR11: Eves 6F 37
Drake St. WR13: Well 4H 31
Drapers Cl. WR4: Warn 1B 18
Draycote Cl. WR5: Worc 4H 21
DRAYCOTT .6G 25

Drift, The WR11: Bad 2C 40
Drinkwater Cl. HR8: Led 2A 42
Drive, The WR2: Pow 6A 20
   WR3: Hind .4D 14
   WR3: Worc .5F 13
Droitwich Community Woods 1A 10
Droitwich Golf Course 3F 9
Droitwich Rd.
   WR3: Clain, Fern H, M Hus, Worc . . .1F 17
   WR9: Omb .5B 6
DROITWICH SPA 6D 8
DROITWICH SPA BMI HOSPITAL 6D 8
Droitwich Spa Heritage Cen. 6D 8
   (off Victoria Sq.)
Droitwich Spa Leisure Cen. 6B 8
Droitwich Spa Station (Rail) 6C 8
Drovers Grn. WR9: D Spa 4B 8
   (off Shepherds Hill)
Drovers Pl. WR9: D Spa 4B 8
Drovers Way WR3: Worc 6A 14
   WR9: D Spa 4B 8
Drumbles La. WR4: Warn 3E 19
Drury La. WR3: M Hus 6A 10
Dryden Cl. WR3: Worc 1G 17
   WR14: Mal .5E 27
Drysdale Cl. WR11: W'ford 6B 40
Duck Mdw. WR4: Warn 3D 18
Dudley Cl. WR2: Worc 4B 16
Dugard Way WR9: D Spa 4C 10
Dugdale Dr. WR4: Warn 4E 19
Duke of Edinburgh Way WR14: Mal 2F 27
Duke's Way WR14: Mal 3F 29
DUNHAMPSTEAD 6H 11
Dunkirk Dr. WR5: B Vill 5C 22
Dunmow Av. WR4: Warn 4E 19
Dunns Copse HR8: Led 5C 42
Dunn's La. WR8: Upt Sev 3C 32
Dunster Cl. WR4: Warn 6D 14
Durcott Gdns. WR11: Eves 2E 39
Durcott Rd. WR11: Eves 2E 39
Durham Rd. WR5: Worc 4C 18
Dutton St. WR3: Worc 1G 5 (3H 17)
Dymock Rd. HR8: Led 5A 42
Dyson Dr. WR14: Mal 6H 27

E

Eagle Cl. WR5: Worc 4G 21
EARL'S CROOME 1E 33
Earlsdon Rd. WR2: Worc 1D 20
Eastabrook Cl. WR14: Mal 2E 27
Eastbank Dr. WR3: Worc 6E 13
Eastbury Mnr. Ct. WR2: Lwr Bro 1B 16
East Cl. WR9: Wych 2E 9
East Comer WR2: Worc 3C 16
Eastfield Cl. WR3: Fern H 2A 14
Eastnor Cl. WR5: Worc 2A 22
East Pk. Dr. WR9: D Spa 5B 8
East St. WR1: Worc 1E 5 (3G 17)
Eastward Rd. WR14: Mal 2D 26
East Waterside WR8: Upt Sev 3C 32
Eastwick Dr. WR11: Eves 3C 38
Easy Row WR1: Worc 2C 4 (4F 17)
Eaton Rd. WR14: Mal W 6C 28
Ebrington Dr. WR4: Warn 6D 14
Ebrington Rd. WR14: W Mal 5A 26
Eden Cl. WR5: Worc 3A 22
Edgar St. WR1: Worc 6E 5 (6G 17)
Edgehill Ct. WR5: Worc 6H 17
   (off Battenhall Wlk.)
Edgeworth Cl. WR4: Warn 1C 18
Edith Berry Cl. WR14: Mal 6F 27
Edith Wlk. WR14: Mal 6D 26
Edmonton Cl. WR2: Worc 3D 20
Edward Cl. WR5: Worc 6H 5 (6H 17)
Edward Hall Ho. WR8: Upt Sev 4C 32
Edward St. WR11: Eves 6D 36
Egghill WR9: D Spa 3C 8
Egg La. WR3: Clain 1F 13
Egremont Gdns. WR4: Warn 2E 19
Elbury Pk. Rd. WR4: Warn 3C 18
Elgar Av. WR14: Mal 5G 27
Elgar Cl. HR8: Led 4A 42
Elgar Cl. WR3: M Hus 5A 10
   WR3: Worc 1G 5 (3H 17)
Elgar Cres. WR3: Worc 3D 10
Elgar Dr. WR5: Kemp 5G 25
Elgar Retail Pk. WR3: Worc 1A 18
Eliot St. WR3: Worc 1G 17
Elizabeth Av. WR3: Worc 4F 13
Elizabeth Cl. HR8: Led 3B 42
Elizabeth Ct. WR9: D Spa 6E 9

Elizabeth Rd. WR11: Eves 3D 38
Elkstone Cl. WR4: Warn 6B 14
Elliot Ct. WR14: Mal 5E 27
Ellison Av. WR2: Worc 2C 16
Ellis Rd. WR2: Worc 6E 17
Ellsdon WR5: Kemp 4G 25
Ellsdon Ri. WR5: Kemp 4G 25
Elm Ct. WR5: Worc 4G 21
Elmdale Rd. WR3: Worc 5F 13
Elmfield WR8: Bau 1H 33
Elmfield Gdns. WR5: Worc 6H 17
Elm Grn. Cl. WR5: Worc 4G 21
Elmley Cl. WR14: Mal 6F 27
Elm Rd. WR2: Worc 2A 4 (4E 17)
   WR11: Eves 1F 39
Elmsdale Rd. HR8: Led 4B 42
Elms Dr. WR13: C Grn 3A 30
Elmside WR11: Eves 1F 39
Eltric Rd. WR3: Worc 5F 13
Ely Cl. WR5: Worc 6C 18
Emerald Rd. WR2: Worc 4C 16
Emes Cl. WR10: Per 5C 34
Emperor Dr. WR5: Worc 4B 22
End Hill Vw. WR14: Mal 2B 26
Engadine Cl. WR14: Mal 4E 29
Enid Blyton Cnr. WR9: D Spa 3C 10
Enigma Bus. Pk. WR14: Mal 3G 27
Enigma Commercial Cen. WR14: Mal 4G 27
Ennerdale Cl. WR2: Worc 2C 18
Enterprise Centre, The WR11: Eves 6F 39
Enterprise Way WR11: Eves 5E 39
Epsom Cl. WR3: Fern H 2B 14
Eskdale Cl. WR2: Worc 2B 18
Essex Cl. WR2: Pow 1A 24
   WR2: Worc .5B 16
Essex Dr. WR3: Fern H 3H 13
Eston Av. WR14: Mal 1G 29
Evendene Rd. WR11: Hamp 1A 38
EVENDINE .4B 30
Evendine Cl. WR5: Worc 1H 21
Evendine La. WR13: C Grn, C Sto 4A 30
Everard Cl. WR2: Worc 2C 16
Everard Pl. WR2: Worc 2C 16
Everoak Ind. Est. WR2: Worc 6C 16
Eversley Cl. WR14: Mal 5F 27
Eversley Gro. WR14: Mal 5F 27
Evertons Cl. WR9: D Spa 2C 10
EVESHAM 5D 36
Evesham Arts Cen. 5E 37
Evesham By-Pass WR11: Eves 3E 37
Evesham Country Pk. 2E 37
EVESHAM COMMUNITY HOSPITAL 2D 38
Evesham Leisure Cen. 2C 38
Evesham Rd. WR10: Lwr Moor, Upp M 2H 35
   WR10: Wick 6G 35
   WR11: Eves, Harv, Nort 2D 36
   WR11: Off .4H 37
   WR12: B'way 3E 41
Evesham Rowing Club 2D 38
Evesham Sailing Club 6E 37
Evesham Shop. Pk. WR11: Eves 5D 36
Evesham Station (Rail) 6D 36
Evesham Trade Cen. WR11: Eves 3D 38
Evesham Vale Light Railway 2E 37
Exbury Pl. WR5: Worc 3A 22
Exeter Rd. WR5: Worc 5C 18

F

Fabricius Av. WR9: D Spa 1D 10
Fairbairn Av. WR3: Worc 6F 13
FAIRFIELD 3C 38
Fairfield Cl. HR8: Led 4B 42
   WR4: Warn .2B 18
Fairfield Pl. WR11: Eves 3D 38
Fairfield Rd. WR11: Eves 3C 38
Fairfields Rd. HR8: Led 4B 42
Fairmount Cl. WR4: Worc 1B 18
Fairmount Rd. WR4: Worc 1B 18
Fairwater Cl. WR11: Eves 2E 39
Fairwater Gdns. WR11: Eves 2E 39
Fairway, The WR4: Warn 3C 18
Fairways WR10: Per 4D 34
Fairways Wlk. WR10: Per 4D 34
Falcon Cl. WR5: Worc 4G 21
   WR9: D Spa 3F 11
Falkland Rd. WR11: Eves 2E 39
Fallow Fld. WR4: Warn 2E 19
Falmouth WR4: Warn 1F 19
FALSAM PITTS 3C 10
Falstaff Dr. WR9: D Spa 3C 10
Farjeon Cl. HR8: Led 3A 42
Farleigh Rd. WR10: Per 6C 34
Farley Rd. WR14: Mal 3F 27

Farley St. WR2: Worc 3C 16
Farlie Cl. WR5: Kemp 5G 25
Farmbank Rd. WR9: Hamp L 2H 7
Farmbrook Cl. WR2: Worc 6A 16
Farm Cl. WR3: Worc 6A 14
Farm Ct. WR12: Will 1H 41
Farmers Ct. WR9: D Spa 4B 8
Farmers Grn. WR9: D Spa 4B 8
Farmers Piece WR9: D Spa 4B 8
(off Farmers Ct.)
Farmers Way WR9: D Spa 4B 8
Farncombe Ter. WR10: Per 6C 34
Farne Av. WR5: Worc 3A 22
Farnham Grn. WR4: Warn 1E 19
Farriers Cl. WR3: Worc 5B 8
Farriers Cnr. WR9: D Spa 5B 8
Farriers Sq. WR9: D Spa 5B 8
(off Farriers Cl.)
Farrier St. WR1: Worc 2D 4 (4F 17)
Farriers Way WR9: D Spa 5B 8
Farrington WR5: B Vill 5B 22
Farundles Av. WR4: Warn 2D 18
Fearnal Ct. WR3: Fern H 2B 14
Fels Av. WR4: Warn 4E 19
Ferndale Cl. WR3: Worc 4E 13
Ferndown Rd. HR8: Led 5B 42
Fern Dr. WR14: Mal 2C 26
Fernhill Gro. WR14: Mal 6E 27
FERNHILL HEATH 2C 14
Fern Rd. WR2: Worc 3C 16
Ferry Bank WR2: Worc 3D 16
Ferry Cl. WR2: Worc 3D 16
Ferry La. WR11: Off 3G 37
Ferry Vw. WR11: Eves 1C 38
Festival Theatre 1D 28
(within Malvern Theatres)
Field Cl. WR3: Worc 1A 18
Fielden Cl. WR11: Eves 2E 39
Fielden Row WR4: Warn 4E 19
Fieldfare Cl. WR14: Mal 1B 26
Fieldhead Cl. WR2: Worc 6B 16
Field Ho. Gdns. WR5: Worc 5G 5 (5H 17)
Field La. WR12: Will 2H 41
Field Rd. WR3: Worc 1A 18
WR4: Worc 1A 18
Field Row WR8: Upt Sev 3C 32
(off Gardens Wlk.)
Fields Cl. WR11: Bad 2C 40
Field Ter. WR5: Worc 1G 21
Field Wlk. WR5: Worc 2H 21
Finch Cl. WR3: Clain 2A 14
Firlands Ct. WR3: Fern H 2B 14
Firlea WR8: Upt Sev 4C 32
(off Church Wlk.)
Firs, The WR5: Kemp 4G 25
WR5: Whitt 5F 23
WR9: D Spa 6B 8
Firs Cl. WR14: Mal 3D 28
First Av. WR2: Worc 2E 21
Fir Tree Rd. WR3: Fern H 2B 14
Fir Tree Wlk. WR14: Mal 3E 27
Fir Way WR4: Worc 1A 18
Fish St. WR1: Worc 5D 4 (5F 17)
Fiskin La. WR4: Warn 4E 19
Fitcher Cl. WR2: Worc 1C 16
Fitzwilliam Cl. WR2: Worc 4A 16
Five Oaks Cl. WR14: Mal 1H 29
Flag Mdw. Wlk. WR1: Worc 2F 17
Flats, The WR10: Per 5C 34
Fleece Rd. WR12: B'way 4G 41
Fleet Row WR5: Worc 3A 22
Fleetwood Av. WR2: Pow 6A 14
Florence Av. WR9: D Spa 2C 10
Florence Cl. WR5: Kemp 5G 25
Foley Rd. WR2: Worc 1D 20
Foley Ter. WR14: Mal 1C 28
Foley Wlk. WR2: Worc 1D 20
Ford Cl. WR14: Mal 1G 29
Ford La. WR9: Elm 3E 9
Foredraught La. WR9: Tib 5H 15
Foregate, The WR1: Worc 3D 4 (4F 17)
Foregate St. WR1: Worc 2D 4 (4F 17)
Forest, The WR9: Hamp L 1B 8
Forest Cl. WR2: Worc 3C 16
Forest Ga. WR11: Eves 3E 39
Fort Royal Ct. WR5: Worc 6H 17
Fort Royal Hill WR5: Worc 6F 5 (6G 17)
Fort Royal La. WR5: Worc 6G 5 (6H 17)
Fort Royal M. WR5: Worc 6F 5
Forum Theatre 1D 28
(within Malvern Theatres)
Fossil Bank WR13: Upp C 6B 28
Foster Dr. WR12: B'way 2G 41
Foster Rd. WR11: Eves 2E 39
Fotheringhay WR4: Warn 1F 19

Foundry All. WR1: Worc 5F 5
Foundry St. WR1: Worc 5F 5 (5G 17)
Fountain Cl. WR11: Eves 2D 38
Fountain Gdns. WR11: Eves 2D 38
Fountain Pl. WR1: Worc 2F 17
FOUR POOLS 4D 38
(not continuous)
Four Pools Ind. Est. WR11: Eves 4C 38
Four Pools La. WR11: Eves 3E 39
(Four Pools Rd.)
WR11: Eves 4E 39
(Spinney Gro.)
Four Pools Retail Pk. WR11: Eves 3E 39
Four Pools Rd. WR11: Eves 3E 39
Fowler Av. WR4: Warn 4E 19
Fox Dr. WR5: Worc 4B 22
Foxes Hill WR5: Kemp 5H 25
Foxglove Cl. WR11: Eves 3F 39
WR14: Mal 2H 29
Foxglove Rd. WR5: Worc 5G 21
Foxhunter Cl. WR9: D Spa 3F 11
Fox La. HR8: Led .3B 42
Foxwell St. WR5: Worc 1A 22
Framlingham Cl. WR5: Worc 3H 21
Frampton Dr. WR12: Will 1H 41
Franklin Cl. WR2: Worc 3D 20
Fraser Cl. WR14: Mal 3E 29
Frederick Rd. WR14: Mal 3D 26
Freemantle Dr. WR5: Kemp 5G 25
Freesia Cl. WR11: Eves 1G 39
French Cl. WR10: Per 4C 34
Friar Cl. WR1: Worc 5E 5
Friar St. WR1: Worc 5E 5 (5G 17)
WR9: D Spa 6D 8
Friary Sq. WR1: Worc 4C 4
Friary Wlk. WR1: Worc 4D 4 (4F 17)
Fridays Acre WR9: D Spa 2B 10
Friends M. WR1: Worc 3E 5
Friesland Cl. WR3: Worc 6H 13
Frobisher Bus. Pk. WR14: Mal 1C 26
Frome Brook Rd. HR8: Led 2A 42
Frost Rd. HR8: Led 2A 42
Fruiterers Arms Caravan Pk. WR9: Uph 3A 6
Fruitlands WR14: Mal W 5C 28
Fry Cl. WR4: Warn 5E 19
Fulbert Rd. WR9: Per 5C 34
Furlong, The WR9: D Spa 4D 8
Furlong Ct. HR8: Led 5B 42
Furlongs Rd. WR8: Upt Sev 5C 32
WR10: Per 3D 34
Furness Rd. WR4: Warn 2B 18

G

Gainsborough Cl. WR13: Well 3G 31
Gala Bingo
Worcester 2D 4 (4F 17)
Gallipoli Dr. WR5: B Vill 5B 22
Galton Way WR9: H'zor 6G 9
Gamekeepers Dr. WR4: Worc 1B 18
Ganderton Ct. WR10: Per 5D 34
Gardeners Cl. WR4: Worc 1B 18
Gardener's Sq. WR11: Eves 1E 39
Gardens Cl. WR8: Upt Sev 4C 32
Gordon Stiles WR10: Per 5C 34
Gardens Wlk. WR8: Upt Sev 3C 32
GARRETT BANK .3H 31
Garth, The HR8: Led 2B 42
Gaudet Luce Golf Course 3G 11
Gawtree Way WR4: Warn 2E 19
Gazala Dr. WR5: B Vill 5B 22
Geneva Av. WR3: Worc 4E 29
Geneva Cl. WR3: Worc 5E 13
Gentian Cl. WR3: Clain 2A 14
Geoffrey Chaucer Wlk. WR9: D Spa 3C 10
George Baylis Rd. WR9: D Spa 5C 8
George La. WR10: Upp M, W Pid 1H 35
George Marshall Medical Mus. 5D 18
George St. WR1: Worc 4F 5 (5G 17)
WR11: Eves 6C 36
Georgina Av. WR2: Worc 1E 21
Geraldine Cl. WH14: Mal 2F 29
Geraldine Ct. WR14: Mal 2F 29
Geraldine Rd. WR14: Mal 1F 29
Gheluvelt Cl. WR1: Worc 2F 17
Gheluvelt M. WR1: Worc 2E 17
Gibbs La. WR1: Off 2G 37
Gibson Gro. WR14: Mal 4C 26
Gibson Rd. HR8: Led 2A 42
Giffard Dr. WR13: Well 3G 31
Gig Bri. La. WR10: Per 3D 34
Gilbert Rd. WR14: Mal 1F 29
Gillam St. WR3: Worc 2G 17
Gilmour Cres. WR3: Worc 5F 13

Glade, The WR14: Mal 6G 27
Glebe Cl. WR2: Worc 5A 4 (5D 16)
Glencoe Rd. WR11: Eves 1F 39
Glendale WR9: D Spa 2B 10
Glenridding Cl. WR4: Warn 2C 18
Glenthorne Av. WR4: Worc 2B 18
Gloucester Cl. WR14: Mal 2G 27
Gloucester Dr. WR11: Eves 6B 24
Gloucester Rd. HR8: Led, Park 4C 42
WR8: Upt Sev 6A 32
WR13: Well 4G 31
Glovers Needle 4D 4 (5F 17)
Goddard Rd. WR3: Worc 2F 17
Golden La. WR11: W'ford 4B 40
Golding Way HR8: Led 1A 42
Goldsmith Rd. WR4: Worc 1B 18
Goodalls Gro. WR11: Eves 5D 36
Goodrest Cl. WR3: Worc 2G 17
Goodrest Wlk. WR3: Worc 2G 17
Goodrich Av. WR4: Worc 1E 19
Goodson Rd. WR14: Mal 2G 27
Goodwin Gdns. WR11: Eves 1E 39
(off Lower Leys)
Goodwood Av. WR5: Worc 1A 22
Goodwood Cl. WR3: Fern H 3B 14
WR5: Worc 1A 22
WR11: Eves 3C 38
Goodwood Grn. WR3: Fern H 3B 14
Goodwood Rd. WR10: Per 1E 35
WR14: Mal 3E 27
Gordon Cl. WR12: B'way 5F 41
Gordon Russell Mus. 5G 41
Gordon Ter. WR14: Mal W 5C 28
Gorse Cl. WR9: D Spa 3E 11
Gorse Hill Rd. WR5: Worc 2B 18
Grafson Pl. WR9: D Spa 2B 10
Grafton Cl. WR14: Mal 4C 26
Graftons, The WR8: Upt Sev 5D 32
Graham Ct. WR14: Mal 6D 26
Graham Rd. WR2: Worc 6D 16
WR14: Mal 6D 26
Grand Stand Rd. WR1: Worc 2A 4 (4E 17)
Grange Av. WR3: Worc 4E 13
Grange La. WR2: R'ick 1A 20
WR3: Clain, Fern H 3H 13
Grange Rd. WR14: Mal 1D 28
Grange Way WR14: Warn 4E 19
Grasmere Dr. WR4: Warn 2C 18
Grasshopper Av. WR5: Worc 4A 22
Grassington Dr. WR4: Warn 3C 18
Grayling Cl. WR5: Worc 4G 21
Great Calcroft WR10: Per 5D 34
Great Ho. Rd. WR2: Worc 6D 16
GREAT MALVERN 5F 27
Great Malvern Priory 1D 28
Great Malvern Station (Rail) 1E 29
Gt. Oaty Gdns. WR1: Worc 1B 18
Gt. Western Bus. Pk. WR4: Worc 1H 5 (3H 17)
Green, The WR2: Hall 4B 12
WR10: Pin 1B 34
WR12: B'way 6F 41
Greenacres Rd. WR2: Worc 5B 16
Greenbank WR9: D Spa 1F 11
Green Cl. WR13: C Grn 4A 30
Greenfield Cl. WR4: Warn 3D 18
Greenfield Path WR14: Mal 5C 26
Greenfields WR0: Upt Cov 4A 32
Greenfields Rd. WR14: Mal 2D 26
Greenford Gdns. WR2: Worc 2C 16
Green Gables Bus. Cen. WR11: Eves 6F 37
Greengate Way WR11: Hamp 3A 38
GREENHILL 5D 36
GREENHILL WR11: Eves 5D 36
Green Hill (Bath Rd.) WR5: Worc 6F 5 (6G 17)
Greenhill Dr. WR14: Mal 6E 27
Greenhill Gdns. WR11: Eves 5D 36
Greenhill Ho. WR11: Eves 5D 36
Greenhill La. WR2: Hall 3B 12
Green Hill (London Rd.)
WR5: Worc 6F 5 (6G 17)
Greenhill Pk. Rd. WR11: Eves 4E 37
Green Hill Pl. WR5: Worc 6F 5 (6G 17)
Greenhill Ter. WR11: Eves 4D 36
Green La. HR8: Led 3C 42
WR3: Bev .3E 13
WR3: Worc 1A 18
WR8: Naun 5H 33
WR8: Rya .1H 31
WR9: H'zor 2G 11
WR14: Mal W 2G 11
Green Leys WR11: Bad 2C 40
GREEN STREET 4G 33
Green St. WR5: Kemp 4H 25
Greenway, The WR2: Pow 6A 20
Gregory's Bank WR3: Worc 2G 17

Gregory's Ct. WR3: Worc 2G 17
Gregory's Mill St. WR3: Worc 1F 17
Grenville Rd. WR2: Worc 5B 16
Gresham Ct. WR1: Worc 2F 17
Gresham Rd. WR2: Worc 4B 16
Gresley Rd. WR4: Warn 6D 14
Greyfriars, The 5E 5
Grisedale Dr. WR4: Warn 1C 18
Grit La. WR14: Mal 1C 26
Grosmont Av. WR4: Warn 1F 19
Grosvenor Bus. Cen. WR11: Eves 5F 39
Grosvenor Cl. WR9: D Spa 2F 11
Grosvenor Cres. WR9: D Spa 2E 11
Grosvenor Wlk. WR2: Worc 5A 4 (5D 16)
Grosvenor Way WR9: D Spa 2E 11
GROVE, THE 3F 33
Grove, The WR3: Worc 4F 13
Grove Cres. WR2: Worc 6B 16
    WR8: Rya 3F 33
Grove Farm WR2: Worc 6A 16
Grove Fld. WR4: Warn 6D 14
Grove Way WR2: R'ick 6A 16
Grovewood Rd. WR14: Mal 3G 27
Grundy's La. WR14: Mal W 2E 31
Guarlford Rd. WR14: Mal 2G 29
Guildford Cl. WR5: Worc 5B 18
Gurneys La. WR9: D Spa 6E 9

H

Habershon Ct. WR9: H'zor 1H 11
HADLEY 5E 7
HADZOR 2H 11
Hadzor La. WR9: H'zor 1F 11
Haggs Mdw. WR4: Warn 2E 19
Hailsham Cl. WR5: Worc 1A 22
Haines Av. WR4: Warn 4E 19
    WR10: W Pid 1G 35
Haines Pl. WR11: Eves 1D 38
Haisley Row WR4: Warn 2E 19
Halas Ho. WR14: Mal W 1E 31
Hales Orchard WR2: Worc 6A 4 (6E 17)
HALFKEY 1B 26
Halfkey Ct. WR14: Mal 1B 26
Halfkey Rd. WR14: Mal 1B 26
Halifax Dr. WR2: Worc 2D 20
Hall Cl. WR4: Warn 2C 18
HALL GREEN 1H 29
Hall Grn. WR8: Upt Sev 5D 32
    WR14: Mal 2H 29
Hall Grn. Cl. WR14: Mal 1H 29
HALLOW 3B 12
HALLOW HEATH 3A 12
Hallow Pk. WR2: Hall 5C 12
Hallow Rd. WR2: Worc 1C 16
Hallwood Dr. HR8: Led 4A 42
Hamble Cl. WR5: Worc 5A 18
Hamilton Cl. WR2: Pow 5A 4
Hamilton Rd. WR5: Worc 5F 5 (5G 17)
    WR11: Eves 3C 38
Hamilton Sq. WR1: Worc 2C 4
Ham La. WR2: Pow 5A 20
Hammond Cl. WR9: D Spa 2E 11
Hammond St. WR9: H'zor 1G 11
Hampden Rd. WR14: Mal 3E 27
HAMPTON 2B 38
Hampton Cl. WR2: Worc 4C 16
Hampton Gdns. WR2: Worc 4C 16
HAMPTON LOVETT 2B 8
Hampton Lovett Ind. Est.
    WR9: Hamp L 2R 8
Hampton Rd. WR9: D Spa 5D 8
Hamptons, The WR9: Omb 4A 6
    (off Wellington Rd.)
Hams Way WR2: R'ick, Pow 1B 20
Ham Vw. WR8: Upt Sev 4C 32
Hanbury Av. WR2: Worc 1D 20
Hanbury Pk. Rd. WR2: Worc 2D 20
Hanbury Rd. WR9: D Spa 6E 9
Hanbury St. WR9: D Spa 6E 9
Hancocks La. WR14: L Mal 6F 31
Handbury Rd. WR14: Mal 6F 31
HANLEY CASTLE 1A 32
Hanley Castle Sports Hall 1A 32
Hanley Rd. WR8: Han C, Upt Sev 2B 32
    WR13: Mal W, Well 1E 31
    WR14: Mal W 4A 32
Hanley Ter. WR14: Mal W 6C 28
Hanson Way WR10: Per 6D 34
Happy Land Nth. WR2: Worc 6D 16
Happy Land W. WR2: Worc 6D 16
Happy Valley WR14: Mal 1C 28
Harbinger Av. WR14: Mal 6F 27
Harbour Dr. WR13: C Sto 1B 30

Harcourt Rd. WR13: C Sto 3A 28
    WR14: W Mal 3A 28
Harden Ct. WR1: Worc 2F 17
    (off Thorneloe Wlk.)
Hardknott Row WR4: Warn 1F 19
Hardwicke Cl. WR2: Worc 3A 4 (4E 17)
Hardy Ct. WR3: Worc 1G 17
Haresfield Cl. WR4: Warn 1B 18
Harlech Cl. WR4: Warn 1E 19
Harlequin Cl. HR8: Led 4A 42
Harling Ct. HR8: Led 3B 42
Harrington Rd. WR2: Worc 6B 16
Harris Cl. WR9: D Spa 6C 8
Harris Hill WR9: D Spa 6D 8
Harrison Cl. WR2: Pow 1A 24
Harrow Cft. WR2: Worc 6A 16
Harry Davis Ct. WR1: Worc 1F 21
Harter Row WR4: Warn 1C 18
Harvey Rd. WR11: Eves 1E 39
Harvey Wlk. WR3: Worc 2H 17
Hasnett Rd. HR8: Led 4A 42
Hastings Dr. WR4: Warn 1E 19
Hastings Pool WR14: Mal 2G 29
Hastings Rd. WR14: Mal 1H 29
Haswell Ho. WR1: Worc 3E 5
Hatfield La. WR5: Nort 6D 22
Hathaway Cl. WR2: Worc 4B 16
HAWFORD 1F 13
Hawford Ho. WR3: Bev 1F 13
Hawford Lock La. WR3: Clain 1E 13
Hawford Pl. WR9: D Spa 2B 10
Hawkesbury Ho. WR11: Eves 1E 39
Hawkins Cl. WR2: Worc 4A 16
Hawkley Row WR4: Warn 3E 19
Hawkshead Ct. WR4: Warn 1D 18
Hawkwood Cl. WR14: Mal 4C 26
Hawkwood Cres. WR2: Worc 3C 16
Hawthorne Wlk. WR9: D Spa 3D 10
Hawthorn La. WR14: Mal 4F 29
Hawthorn Rd. WR4: Worc 1H 5 (3A 18)
    WR11: Eves 3F 39
Hay Cl. WR4: Warn 3C 18
Haye La. WR9: H'ley, Omb 4B 6
Hayes Bank Rd. WR14: Mal 4F 29
Hayfield Cl. WR2: Worc 6B 16
Hay La. WR9: H'zor, Sha G 4H 11
Hayling Cl. WR5: Worc 3A 22
Haynes Ct. WR14: Mal 2F 27
Hays Cl. WR12: Will 2H 41
Haysfield, The WR14: Mal 3G 27
Hayslan Av. WR14: Mal 5F 27
Hayslan Grn. WR14: Mal 5F 27
Hayslan Rd. WR14: Mal 5F 27
Haywain Av. WR4: Warn 2E 19
Haze Cft. WR4: Warn 3D 18
Hazel Av. WR11: Eves 3F 39
Hazel Cl. WR4: Worc 2B 18
    WR9: D Spa 3D 10
Hazelwood Cl. WR5: Worc 6B 18
Hazle Cl. HR8: Led 5B 42
Head St. WR10: Per 5D 34
Heath Cl. WR2: Hall 2B 12
Heath Dr. WR5: Worc 4A 22
Heather Cl. WR5: Worc 5G 21
Heathers, The WR11: Eves 5D 38
Heathlands Cl. WR14: Mal W 4E 31
Heath Ter. WR2: Hall 2A 12
Hebb St. WR1: Worc 3F 17
Heights, The WR5: Worc 4D 18
Helford Cl. WR2: Worc 5A 18
Hemmingway WR11: Eves 3D 38
Hemsby Cl. WR6: Worc 3H 21
Hemsley Pl. WR2: Warn 1E 19
HENBROOK 1F 9
Henley Dr. WR9: D Spa 2E 11
Henley Pl. WR14: Mal 4D 26
Henry Fowler Cl.
    WR11: Eves 6D 36
Henry St. WR1: Worc 2F 17
    WR11: Eves 1C 38
Henwick Av. WR2: Worc 4D 16
Henwick Cl. WR2: Worc 4A 4 (5E 17)
Henwick Gro. WR2: Worc 3C 16
Henwick Ho. WR2: Worc 4C 16
    (Packhorse Cl.)
    WR2: Worc 5A 4
    (St Clement's Cl.)
Henwick Pde. WR2: Worc 1A 4 (3D 16)
Henwick Rd. WR2: Worc 2A 4 (2D 16)
Hereford Rd. HR8: Led 1A 42
Heriotts Ct. WR9: D Spa 6E 9
Heriotts La. WR9: D Spa 6E 9
    (not continuous)
Heritage Way WR9: D Spa 6D 8
Herne Fld. WR4: Warn 2E 19

Heron Cl. WR2: Worc 3E 21
Heron Pl. WR9: D Spa 6F 9
Herriotts, The WR9: D Spa 6E 9
Hetherington Cl. WR5: Kemp 4G 25
Hetherington Ri. WR4: Warn 4E 19
Hever Av. WR4: Warn 1E 19
Heywell Wlk. WR14: Mal 1D 28
Hidcote Cl. WR5: Worc 4H 21
Highfield WR2: C End 4D 24
Highfield Cl. WR9: D Spa 1D 10
    WR14: Mal 3E 27
Highfield Rd. WR11: Hamp 1B 38
    WR14: Mal 3D 26
Highgate Ct. WR12: B'way 5F 41
Highland Rd. WR4: Worc 3A 18
Highlea WR14: Mal 1D 28
High Pk. WR5: Whitt 5F 23
High St. HR8: Led 3C 42
    WR1: Worc 4D 4 (5F 17)
    WR8: Upt Sev 3C 32
    WR9: D Spa 6D 8
    WR10: Per 4D 34
    WR11: Bad 2B 40
    WR11: Eves 1D 38
    WR12: B'way 5F 41
Hill Av., The WR5: Worc 1G 21
Hillcarinie Ho. WR9: D Spa 6D 8
    (off St Andrew's Rd.)
Hill Centre, The 4A 32
Hill Cl. WR10: Per 4C 34
Hillcrest WR11: Eves 2F 39
Hillcrest Ri. WR3: Worc 4E 13
HILL END 5E 9
Hillend WR9: D Spa 5E 9
    (off Bromsgrove Rd.)
Hillery Rd. WR5: Worc 1B 22
Hillfield Dr. HR8: Led 2C 42
Hillsfield WR8: Upt Sev 4C 32
Hillside WR5: Kemp 3G 25
    WR11: Ald 6H 37
Hillside Cl. WR5: Worc 4B 18
    WR11: Hamp 2A 38
    WR14: Mal W 4C 28
Hillstone Ct. WR14: Mal 6D 26
Hill St. WR5: Worc 3G 5 (5H 17)
Hill Top La. WR9: Omb 5B 6
Hill Vw. Cl. WR13: C Sto 1B 30
    WR14: Mal 2F 27
Hillview Dr. WR14: Mal 3C 26
Hillview Gdns. WR8: Rya 3E 33
Hill Vw. Rd. WR2: Worc 2D 20
    WR14: Mal 2C 26
Hill Wlk. WR14: Mal 5D 26
Hill Wood Cl. WR4: Warn 3D 18
Hilton Rd. WR14: Mal 2G 29
Himbleton Ho. WR2: Worc 3C 16
Himbleton Rd. WR2: Worc 3C 16
HINDLIP 4D 14
Hindlip La. WR3: Hind 4H 13
    (not continuous)
Hingley Av. WR4: Warn 4D 18
Hipkiss Gdns. WR9: D Spa 5C 8
Hither Grn. WR11: Bad 1C 40
Hobhouse Gdns. WR4: Warn 4E 19
Hock Coppice WR4: Warn 3D 18
Hodges, The WR11: Eves 6D 36
Hodges Yd. HR8: Led 3B 42
    (off The Homend)
Holdings La. WR5: Kemp 2H 25
Holland Grn. WR4: Warn 4E 19
Hollies, The WR3: Worc 3H 17
    (off Rainbow Hill)
Hollies Mews, The WR14: Mal 2F 27
Holloway WR10: Per 4B 34
Holloway, The WR9: D Spa 6E 9
Holloway Dr. WR10: Per 4B 34
Hollybush Cl. WR14: Mal 2C 26
Holly Cl. WR9: D Spa 3E 11
    WR11: Eves 3F 39
HOLLY GREEN 3E 33
Holly Gro. WR8: Rya 3E 33
Hollyhock Cl. WR11: Eves 2G 39
Holly Mt. WR4: Worc 3A 18
Holly Mt. Rd. WR4: Worc 3A 18
Holly Tree La. WR2: R'ick 1A 20
Holly Vw. Dr. WR14: Mal 4C 28
Holmwood Gdns. WR11: Eves 3F 39
Holt Fleet Rd. WR9: Omb 5A 6
Holywell Hill WR2: Worc 2A 4 (4D 16)
Holywell Rd. WR14: Mal W 4E 31
Homefield Rd. WR2: Worc 6E 17
Homenash Ho. WR1: Worc 2F 17
Homend, The HR8: Led 2B 42
Homend Cres. HR8: Led 2B 42
Homend Trad. Est. HR8: Led 1C 42

Homend Wlk. *HR8: Led* 3B **42**
   (off The Homend)
Home Piece WR9: D Spa 1B **10**
Homesmith Ho. WR11: Eves 6D **36**
Homestead WR9: D Spa 2B **10**
Homestead Av. WR4: Warn 6D **14**
Homestead Cl. WR14: Mal W 4E **31**
Honeymans Gdns. WR9: D Spa 5C **8**
Honeysuckle Cl. WR11: Eves 4D **38**
Honeywood Rd. WR2: Worc 3C **16**
Honister Dr. WR4: Warn 1C **18**
Hood St. WR1: Worc 4C **4** (5F **17**)
Hop Gdns., The WR11: Ald 1B **40**
Hopkiln Gdns. WR11: Eves 1D **38**
Hopmarket, The WR1: Worc 3D **4** (4G **17**)
Hopton Cl. HR8: Led 2A **42**
Hopton St. WR2: Worc 5C **16**
Hop Warehouse, The WR1: Worc 1E **5**
Hornbli Meadows (Nature Reserve) 6E **19**
Hornsby Av. WR4: Warn 4E **19**
Hornyold Av. WR14: Mal 4C **26**
Hornyold Ct. WR14: Mal W 1E **31**
Hornyold Rd. WR14: Mal 4C **26**
Horsebridge Av. WR11: Bad 1B **40**
Horse La. Orchard HR8: Led 3C **42**
Horsford Rd. WR2: Worc 2D **16**
Horton La. WR9: Hamp L 1F **7**
Hoskyns Av. WR4: Warn 4E **19**
Hospital Bank WR14: Mal 4C **26**
Hospital La. WR2: Pow 1A **24**
Hospital Rd. WR14: Mal 1B **26**
Howard Rd. WR2: Worc 1B **18**
Howcroft Grn. WR4: Warn 1D **18**
Howlett Pl. WR4: Warn 4E **19**
Howsell Rd. WR14: Mal 3D **26**
Howsell Rd. Ind. Est. WR14: Mal 3E **27**
Howsells, The WR14: Mal 1F **27**
Hudson Cl. WR2: Worc 2D **20**
   WR10: Per 4C **34**
Humber Rd. WR5: Worc 4A **18**
Hungerpit Wlk. WR3: Worc 1F **17**
Hunstanton Cl. WR5: Worc 3H **21**
Hunt Av. WR4: Warn 3E **19**
Hunter Ri. WR10: Per 5C **34**
Hunters Cl. WR9: D Spa 5B **8**
Hunters End WR9: D Spa 5B **8**
Hunters Grn. WR9: D Spa 5B **8**
Hunters Pl. WR9: D Spa 5B **8**
Hunters Way WR9: D Spa 5B **8**
Huntingdon Hall 4D **4** (5F **17**)
Huntings, The *WR12: B'way* 6G **41**
   (off Church La.)
Hurst La. WR3: Fern H, Hind 3B **14**
Hurst Pk. Cotts. WR10: Per 2E **35**
Hurst Rd. WR10: Per 3D **34**
Huxleys Way WR11: Eves 1C **38**
   (not continuous)
Huxtable Ri. WR4: Warn 3D **18**
Hyacinth Cl. WR5: Worc 5G **21**
   WR11: Eves 1G **39**
Hydefields WR8: Upt Sev 4A **32**
Hyde La. WR8: Upt Sev 4A **32**
Hydrangea Cl. WR5: Worc 5H **21**
Hylton Rd. WR2: Worc 1A **4** (3D **16**)
   WR11: Hamp 1A **38**
Hylton Rd. Trad. Est. WR2: Worc . .3A **4** (4E **17**)

I

Idleton WR4: Warn 4E **19**
Ilkley Cl. WR4: Warn 3C **18**
Imperial Rd. WR14: Mal 1E **29**
Impney Grn. WR9: D Spa 6F **9**
Impney Way WR9: D Spa 6F **9**
Inches La. WR11: Eves 6D **36**
Inett Way WR9: D Spa 6A **8**
Infirmary Wlk. WR1: Worc 2C **4** (4F **17**)
Ingles Dr. WR2: Worc 5A **4** (5D **16**)
Isaacs Way WR9: D Spa 4D **10**
Isaac Wlk. WR2: Worc 6C **16**
Isbourne Cres. WH11: Eves 3D **38**
Ivy La. WR3: Fern H 3C **14**
Ivy St. WR3: Worc 1E **17**

J

Jackdaw La. WR9: D Spa 3F **11**
Jacob Cl. WR3: Worc 6A **14**
Jacobs Ladder WR3: Clain 1H **13**
Jamaica Cres. WR14: Mal 2E **27**
Jamaica Rd. WR14: Mal 3E **27**
James Cl. WR1: Worc 4F **5** (5G **17**)
Jasmine Cl. WR5: Worc 4H **21**

Jasmine Rd. WR14: Mal W 5D **28**
Jasmine Wlk. WR11: Eves 4D **38**
Jasper Rd. WR2: Worc 2D **20**
Jennet Tree La. WR2: C End 4A **24**
Jenny Lind Gro. WR14: Mal 4D **26**
John Comyn Dr. WR3: Clain 5G **13**
John Gwynn Ho. WR1: Worc 4C **4**
John Lee Rd. HR8: Led 3A **42**
John Martin Sq. WR11: Hamp 2B **38**
Joiners Cl. WR4: Warn 1B **18**
Jordans Cl. WR12: Will 2H **41**
Jubilee Cl. HR8: Led 5C **42**
Jubilee Dr. WR13: Upp C 5C **30**
Jubilee Ho. WR3: Worc 2H **17**
Jubilee Rd. WR2: Worc 1E **21**
Jubilee Way WR14: Mal 2C **26**
Juniper Way WR14: Mal W 5D **28**

K

Katharines Wlk. HR8: Led 5B **42**
Keats Av. WR3: Worc 1G **17**
Keble Cl. WR4: Worc 2H **5** (4A **18**)
Kempley Brook Dr. HR8: Led 2B **42**
KEMPSEY 4G **25**
Kempton Cl. WR11: Eves 3C **38**
Kempton Rd. WR10: Per 1F **35**
Kendal Grn. WR4: Warn 1D **18**
Kendall St. WR3: Worc 1G **5** (3H **17**)
Kenilworth Cl. WR3: Worc 1F **5** (3G **17**)
Kenilworth Ct. WR3: Worc 1F **5**
Kennel La. WR12: B'way 6G **41**
Kennels La. WR3: Clain, Fern H 1B **14**
Kennet Grn. WR5: Worc 4H **5** (5A **18**)
Kent Cl. WR11: Hamp 2B **38**
Kentmere Cl. WR4: Warn 2C **18**
   WR14: Mal 1G **27**
Kenwood Av. WR4: Warn 3B **18**
Kenwood Cl. WR4: Warn 3B **18**
Kepax Gdns. WR3: Worc 1E **17**
Keren Dr. WR5: B Vill 6B **22**
Kerry Hill WR3: Worc 5A **14**
Kestrel Cres. WR9: D Spa 4F **11**
Kestrel Dr. WR5: Worc 4G **21**
Keswick Dr. WR4: Warn 1C **18**
Ketch Caravan Pk. WR5: Worc 5G **21**
Key Av. WR4: Warn 4E **19**
Keytec 7 Bus. Pk. WR10: Per 1F **35**
Keytes La. WR12: B'way 6G **41**
Kidderminster Rd. WR9: D Spa, Hamp L 2B **8**
Kielder Ri. WR2: Worc 3D **20**
Kilbury Dr. WR5: Worc 2C **22**
King Arthur's Cl. WR2: Worc 3D **16**
King Charles Av. WR2: Pow 1A **24**
King Charles Cl. WR5: Worc 6F **5**
   WR11: Eves 1D **38**
   (off Vine St.)
King Charles Pl. WR2: Worc 6A **4**
King Edmund Sq. WR1: Worc 2C **4**
King Edward's Rd. WR14: Mal W 5C **28**
Kingfisher Cl. WR5: Worc 3H **21**
Kingfisher Ct. *WR9: D Spa* 6E **9**
   (off Woodfield Rd.)
King George Av. WR9: D Spa 2D **10**
King George's Way WR10: Per 4D **34**
Kingjohns Sq. WR1: Worc 2C **4**
Kingsbury Rd. WR2: Worc 1D **20**
Kings Ct. Bus. Pk. WR5: Worc 5D **18**
Kingsdale Ct. WR12: B'way 5H **41**
KING'S END 5A **20**
King's End Rd. WR2: Pow 5A **20**
King's Hill WR5: Kemp 3G **25**
Kingshill Cl. WR14: Mal 6E **27**
Kingsmead HR8: Led 2A **42**
Kings Rd. WR11: Eves 1F **39**
   WR14: Mal W 4E **31**
King Stephen's Mt. WR2: Worc 2D **16**
Kingston Av. WR3: Worc 1H **17**
Kingston Cl. WR9: D Spa 3E **11**
King St. WR1: Worc 6E **5** (6G **17**)
Kingswood Rd. WR9: Hamp L 2A **8**
Kinnersley Rd. WR14: Mal 1C **26**
Kinord Cl. WR5: Worc 3A **22**
Kipling Cl. WR3: Worc 1G **17**
   WR14: Mal 5E **27**
Kirkby Gdns. WR4: Warn 1C **18**
Kirkham Ho. WR3: Clain 5G **13**
Kirkstone Ct. WR4: Warn 2B **18**
Kleve Wlk. WR1: Worc 5D **4** (5F **17**)
Knapp, The WR11: Bad 2B **40**
Knapp Cl. HR8: Led 2B **42**
Knapp La. HR8: Led 2B **42**
Knapp Pl. WR5: Worc 3A **22**
Knapp Ridge HR8: Led 2C **42**

Knapp Way WR14: Mal 3D **26**
Knightbridge Pk. WR4: Warn 6E **15**
Knight St. WR2: Worc 5D **16**
Knoll La. WR14: Mal 3G **29**
Knotts Av. WR4: Warn 3E **19**
KNOWLE HILL 2A **40**
Kohima Dr. WR5: B Vill 5B **22**

L

Labrador Rd. WR2: Worc 3D **20**
Laburnum Dr. WR11: Eves 4F **39**
Laburnum Rd. WR4: Worc 3A **18**
Laburnum Wlk. WR8: Upt Sev 4C **32**
   WR14: Mal 4D **26**
Lady De Walden Dr.
   WR14: Mal, W Mal 6B **26**
Ladygo La. WR2: Hall 3A **12**
Lady Somerset Dr. HR8: Led 2A **42**
Ladywood Rd. WR9: Lady, Salw 4A **10**
Lahn Dr. WR9: D Spa 3B **10**
Lamb Bank WR14: W Mal 5A **26**
Lambert Rd. WR14: Mal 5D **16**
Lambourne Av. WR14: Mal 2E **27**
Lambourne Cres. WR2: Worc 1C **16**
Lancaster Cl. WR8: Upt Sev 5D **32**
Lancelott Ct. WR10: Per 4C **34**
Lancing Cl. WR5: Worc 1A **22**
Lane Ho. WR3: Fern H 2A **14**
Lane's End WR5: Kemp 4F **25**
Lanesfield Pk. WR11: Eves 5E **37**
Langdale Cl. WR4: Warn 1C **18**
Langdale Dr. WR4: Warn 2B **18**
Langdale Rd. WR1: Worc 2E **17**
Langland, The HR8: Led 2A **42**
Langland Av. WR14: Mal 5G **27**
Langland Cl. WR14: Mal 6G **27**
Langley Cl. WR2: Worc 2C **16**
Langley Rd. WR9: D Spa 2D **10**
Lankets, The WR11: Bad 2C **40**
Lansdowne Cl. WR14: Mal 6F **27**
Lansdowne Ct. WR1: Worc 3F **17**
   WR11: Eves 2E **39**
   (off Port St.)
Lansdowne Cres. WR3: Worc 1F **5** (3G **17**)
   WR14: Mal 6E **27**
Lansdowne Cres. La. WR3: Worc . . .1F **5** (3G **17**)
Lansdowne Flats *WR11: Eves* 2E **39**
   (off Port St.)
Lansdowne Ho. WR14: Mal 6E **27**
Lansdowne M. *WR11: Eves* 2E **39**
   (off Port St.)
Lansdowne Ri. WR3: Worc 3G **17**
Lansdowne Rd. WR1: Worc 3F **17**
   WR3: Worc 3F **17**
   WR14: Mal 3D **26**
Lansdowne Row *WR14: Mal* 3F **17**
   (off Madresfield Rd.)
Lansdowne St. WR1: Worc 3F **17**
Lansdowne Ter. WR1: Worc 3G **17**
   WR14: Mal 6E **27**
Lansdowne Wlk. WR3: Worc 1G **5** (3H **17**)
   (not continuous)
Lapal Cl. WR2: Worc 5A **4** (5D **16**)
Larches, The *WR9: D Spa* 1D **10**
Larchfield Cl. WR14: Mal 3D **26**
Larch Rd. WR4: Worc 1H **5** (3H **17**)
   WR11: Eves 3F **39**
Lark Hill WR5: Worc 6A **18**
Lark Hill Rd. WR5: Worc 6A **18**
Larkspur Dr. WR11: Eves 4C **38**
Larkspur Rd. WR5: Worc 4H **21**
Laslett's Almshouses WR1: Worc 5E **5**
Laslett St. WR1: Worc 2H **17**
Laugherne Rd. WR2: Worc 4D **16**
Launceston Pl. WR4: Warn 1E **19**
Laurel Av. WR11: Eves 3F **39**
Laurel Cl. WR4: Worc 2A **18**
Laurels Av. WR11: Off 3H **37**
Laurels Rd. WR11: Off 3H **37**
Laurelwood Cl. WR9: D Spa 3F **11**
Laurelwood Rd. WR9: D Spa 3E **11**
Lavender Rd. WR3: Worc 1E **17**
Lavender Wlk. WR11: Eves 5C **38**
   WR14: Mal 2G **29**
Lawnside WR14: Mal 1E **29**
Lawnside Cl. WR8: Upt Sev 5A **32**
Lawnside Rd. WR14: Mal 3B **42**
Lawson Cl. WR8: Upt Sev 5D **32**
Laxton Av. WR2: Worc 2C **16**
Layland Wlk. WR5: Worc 1F **21**
Layton Av. WR14: Mal 4F **27**
Leabank Dr. WR3: Worc 4E **13**

Lea Cl. WR3: Worc 4F 13
Leadon Bank HR8: Led 2B 42
Leadon Pl. HR8: Led 5A 42
Leadon Rd. WR14: Mal 1H 29
Leadon Way HR8: Led 4A 42
Lea Hill Cl. WR14: Mal 5D 26
Leamington Ct. WR14: Mal W 3E 31
Leamington Rd. WR12: B'way, Will 3G 41
Lear Cl. WR2: Worc 4B 16
Leas Ho's. WR1: Worc 3C 4
Leasowe Cl. WR2: Worc 6B 16
Leasowes, The HR8: Led 1A 42
Leasowes Rd. WR11: Off 3H 37
Lechmere Cres. WR2: Worc 2C 16
 WR14: Mal 2A 18
Leckhampton Cl. WR4: Warn 6C 14
LEDBURY 3B 42
LEDBURY COMMUNITY HEALTH CARE CENTRE
 . . . . .3B 42
Ledbury Ct. WR14: Mal 2C 26
 (off Hill Vw. Rd.)
Ledbury Heritage Cen. & Gallery 3C 42
Ledbury Leisure Cen. 4C 42
Ledbury Pk. HR8: Led 3C 42
Ledbury Station (Rail) 1B 42
Ledbury Swimming Pool 3B 42
Ledwych Cl. WR9: D Spa 6B 8
Ledwych Gdns. WR9: D Spa 6C 8
Ledwych Rd. WR9: D Spa 6C 8
Leeds Av. WR4: Warn 2E 19
Lees, The WR14: Mal 3D 28
Leicester Gro. WR11: Eves 6D 36
Leicester St. WR1: Worc 3F 17
Leigh Gro. WR9: D Spa 5C 8
Leigh Sinton Rd. WR14: Mal 1C 26
LENCHWICK 1D 36
Leopard Ri. WR5: Worc 4D 18
Leslie Av. WR3: Worc 4E 13
Leven Dr. WR5: Worc 3A 22
Lewes Gdns. WR4: Warn 1E 19
Leycroft WR9: D Spa 2F 11
Ley Orchard WR12: Will 1H 41
Leys, The WR11: Eves 1E 39
Leys Wlk. WR11: Eves 1E 39
Lichfield Av. WR5: Worc 5B 18
 WR11: Eves 6F 37
Lido, The
 Droitwich Spa 6E 9
Lifford Gdns. WR12: B'way 5F 41
Lilac Av. WR4: Worc 1H 5 (3A 18)
Lilac Cl. WR8: Upt Sev 4C 32
 WR9: D Spa 3E 11
 WR11: Hamp .3B 38
Lime Av. WR4: Worc 1A 18
Lime Gro. WR13: Well 3G 31
Limes, The WR5: Kemp 3G 25
Lime St. WR11: Eves 1E 39
Lime Tree Av. WR12: B'way 4H 41
 WR14: Mal W .5C 28
Lincoln Grn. WR5: Worc 6B 18
Linden Cl. WR11: Eves 3F 39
Linden Rd. WR4: Worc 2B 18
 (Hazel Cl.)
 WR4: Worc 2A 18
 (Sycamore Rd.)
Lindsey Av. WR11: Eves 2E 39
Lingfield Rd. WR11: Eves 3C 38
Lingmell Ct. WR4: Warn 1E 19
 (off Martindale Cl.)
Link Elm Cl. WR2: Worc 2D 20
Link Ind. Est. WR14: Mal 3E 27
Link Rd. WR11: Eves 4E 30
Linksview Cres. WR5: Worc 5C 18
Link Ter. WR14: Mal 5D 26
LINK TOP 5C 26
Link Way WR14: Mal 3E 27
Linley Cl. WR3: Worc 4E 13
Lion Ct. WR1: Worc 2E 5 (4G 17)
Lion Wlk. WR1: Worc 2E 5 (4G 17)
Lismore Grn. WR5: Worc 3A 22
Lister Av. WR4: Warn 4E 19
Lit. Boughton St. WR2: Worc 6C 16
Lit. Chestnut St. WR1: Worc 1E 5 (3G 17)
LITTLE EASTBURY 1C 16
Little Hill WR9: D Spa 1A 10
Lit. Hill Ct. WR9: D Spa 1B 10
Lit. Hill Grn. WR9: D Spa 1B 10
 (off Little Hill)
Lit. Holywell Hill WR2: Worc 2A 4 (4D 16)
Little London WR1: Worc 4F 17
LITTLE MALVERN 5E 31
Little Malvern Court 6D 30
Little Malvern Priory 6E 31
Lit. Marcle Ind. Est. HR8: Led 4A 42
Lit. Marcle Rd. HR8: Led 4A 42

Little Orchard WR9: D Spa 1C 10
 (off Wych Rd.)
Little Park WR9: D Spa 1B 10
 (off Padgewell Hill)
Lit. Park St. WR5: Worc 5F 5 (5G 17)
Lit. Penny Rope WR10: Per 6C 34
Little Piece WR4: Warn 2D 18
Lit. Priest La. WR10: Per 5D 34
Lit. Southfield St. WR1: Worc 2E 5 (4G 17)
Littleworth St. WR1: Worc 1D 38
Littleworth Wlk. WR11: Eves 1D 38
Liverpool Rd. WR5: Worc 6B 18
Livingstone St. WR5: Worc 1A 22
Lobelia Cl. WR5: Worc 4H 21
Lock St. WR5: Worc 5F 5 (5G 17)
Lock Vw. WR11: Eves 1E 39
Lockyear Cl. WR13: C Sto 2B 30
Loden Brook Cl. HR8: Led 2B 42
Lodge Cl. WR2: Worc 3C 16
Lodge Dr. WR14: Mal 5C 26
Lofts, The WR1: Worc 1F 5
London La. WR5: Upt Sev 3C 32
London Rd. WR5: Worc 6F 5 (6G 17)
Long Acres HR8: Led 3B 42
Long Bank WR9: D Spa 3C 8
Longdon Ct. WR11: W'ford 4H 39
LONGDON HEATH 6A 32
Longdon Hill WR11: W'ford 4H 39
Longfellow Rd. WR3: Worc 1G 17
Longfield WR8: Upt Sev 4C 32
Longheadland WR9: Omb 4A 6
Long Hedges WR10: Per 6B 34
Longridge Rd. WR14: Mal 4E 29
Long Sling WR9: D Spa 2B 10
Longthorpe WR4: Warn 1E 19
Lord's Heath WR4: Warn 2D 18
Loughmill Rd. WR10: Per 4C 34
Love's Gro. WR1: Worc 2C 4 (4F 17)
Lovett Pl. WR4: Warn 3E 19
Lovett Rd. WR9: Hamp L 2B 8
Lovington La. WR2: Lwr Bro . . . . . .6A 12 & 1A 16
Lowell St. WR1: Worc 1F 5 (3G 17)
Lwr. Barbourne Ter. WR1: Worc 2E 17
Lwr. Bull Entry WR1: Worc 4D 4 (5F 17)
Lwr. Chase Rd. WR14: Mal 1F 29
Lwr. Chestnut St. WR1: Worc 1E 5 (3G 17)
Lower Dingle WR14: W Mal 1A 28
Lwr. Ferry La. WR2: C End 3D 24
Lower Fld. Ter. WR5: Worc 1G 21
Lwr. Grn. WR12: B'way 5F 41
LOWER HOWSELL 1F 27
Lwr. Howsell Rd. WR14: Mal 1F 27
Lower Leys WR11: Eves 1E 39
Lower Meadow WR9: D Spa 1C 10
 (off Wych Rd.)
Lwr. Montpelier Rd. WR14: W Mal 1A 28
Lwr. Priest La. WR10: Per 5D 34
Lwr. Quest Hills Rd. WR14: Mal 3D 26
Lower Rd. HR8: Led 4A 42
 WR14: W Mal .5A 26
Lower Rd. Trad. Est. HR8: Led 3A 42
Lower Smite Farm Nature Reserve 2G 15
LOWER TOWN 1A 14
LOWER WICK 3D 20
Lower Wick Swimming Pool & Health Hydro
 . . . . .3E 21
LOWER WYCHE .4C 28
Lwr. Wyche Rd. WR14: Mal W 4C 28
Lowesmoor WR1: Worc 3E 5 (4G 17)
Lowesmoor Ho. WR1: Worc 2F 5
Lowesmoor Pl. WR1: Worc 2F 5 (4G 17)
Lowesmoor Ter. WR1: Worc 2F 5 (4G 17)
Lowesmoor Wharf WR1: Worc 2F 5 (4G 17)
Low Fold Cl. WR2: Worc 6B 16
Lucerne Av. WR14: Mal 4E 29
Lucerne Cl. WR3: Worc 4E 13
Ludlow Av. WR4: Warn 1D 18
Ludstock Cl. WR5: Worc 1D 22
Lugano Rd. WR5: Worc 5E 13
Lugg Flds. HR8: Led 2A 42
Lundy Row WR5: Worc 3A 22
Lunns Gdns. WR11: Hamp 2B 38
Lutterworth Cl. WR4: Warn 3B 18
Lychgate WR1: Worc 5E 5
Lydes Rd. WR14: Mal 5D 26
Lydford Ter. WR4: Warn 1E 19
Lyf's La. WR5: Kemp 4E 25
Lygon Bank WR14: Mal 5D 26
Lygon Wlk. WR4: Worc 3E 19
Lyndon Bus. Pk. HR8: Led 3A 42
Lyneham Cl. WR4: Warn 6B 14
Lynwood Cl. WR11: Hamp 1B 38
Lyttelton Cl. WR9: D Spa 1E 11
Lyttelton Rd. WR9: D Spa 2D 10

Lyttelton St. WR1: Worc 2E 17
Lyttleton Rd. WR10: Per 1E 35
Lyttleton Sq. WR14: Mal 3E 27

M

Mabbs Cl. WR4: Warn 3E 19
Mabel's Furlong HR8: Led 5C 42
Macaulay Av. WR14: Mal 5E 27
McCormick Av. WR4: Warn 4E 19
McIntyre Rd. WR2: Worc 5C 16
Mackenzie Cl. WR2: Worc 3D 20
McKenzie Way WR4: Worc 2H 5 (4H 17)
McNaught Pl. WR1: Worc 1D 4 (3F 17)
Madresfield Rd. WR13: Mal 6G 27
 WR14: Mal 6E 27
Magdala Cl. WR1: Worc 3C 4
Magistrates' Court
 Worcester 2C 4 (4F 17)
Magnolia Cl. WR5: Worc 4H 21
Magpie Cl. WR5: Worc 4H 21
Main Rd. WR2: Hall 2B 12
 WR5: Kemp 2G 25
 WR9: Omb 2A 6
 WR10: W Pid .2H 35
Main St. WR10: Pin 3A 34
 WR11: Ald 6H 37
 WR11: Off 2G 37
 WR12: Will 1H 41
Malham Pl. WR5: Worc 3A 22
Malinshill Rd. WR11: Hamp 2A 38
Mallard Cl. WR2: Worc 3E 21
Mallard Pl. WR9: D Spa 6F 9
Mallow Cl. WR14: Mal 6E 29
Malthouse Pl. WR1: Worc 4D 4 (5F 17)
Malton Cl. WR14: Mal 1C 26
Malvern Bus. Cen. WR14: Mal 3G 27
Malvern Cinema .1D 28
Malvern College Sports Complex 2E 29
MALVERN COMMON 4F 29
MALVERN COMMUNITY HOSPITAL 4E 27
Malvern Hills Indoor Bowls Club 6E 27
 (within Manor Pk. Sports Club)
Malvern Hills Outdoor Education Cen. 5A 26
Malvern Hills Science Pk. WR14: Mal 2F 29
MALVERN LINK .3E 27
Malvern Link Station (Rail) 3E 27
Malvern Meadows Caravan Site
 WR8: Han S 5G 29
Malvern Mus. of Local History 1D 28
Malvern Rd. WR2: Pow 6A 20
 WR2: Pow, Worc 6A 4 (1D 20)
Malvern Shop. Pk. WR14: Mal 2G 27
Malvern Splash Leisure Complex 1D 28
Malvern Technology Cen. WR14: Mal 3F 29
Malvern Theatres, The 1D 28
Malvern Vw. WR5: Worc 5C 18
MALVERN WELLS 2E 31
Manby Rd. WR14: Mal 1E 29
Mandalay Dr. WR5: B Vill 5B 22
Manitoba Cl. WR2: Worc 3C 20
Manning Pl. WR14: Mal 3E 5
Manning Rd. WR9: D Spa 1C 10
Manor Cl. WR9: D Spa 6E 9
 WR11: Bad 2B 40
 WR11: Bad 5B 40
Manor Farm WR10: W Pid 1H 35
Manor Gdns. WR10: Per 6E 35
 WR11: Ald 1A 40
Manor Pk. Sports Club 6E 27
Manor Pk. Squash Club 6E 27
 (within Manor Pk. Sports Club)
Manor Rd. WR2: Worc 1D 20
 WR11: W'ford .6B 40
Manorside WR11: Bad 2B 40
Mansfield Rd. WR14: Mal 4G 27
Mansion Gdns. WR11: Eves 2D 38
Mapit Pl. WR4: Warn 3E 19
Maple Av. WR4: Worc 3A 18
 WR10: Per 4D 34
Maple Cl. WR11: Eves 3F 39
Maple Gro. WR9: D Spa 3D 10
Maple Rd. WR14: Mal 4G 27
Mapson Cl. WR9: H'zor 1G 11
Margaret Rd. WR14: Mal 3B 42
 WR2: Worc 1E 21
Marhon Cl. WR9: D Spa 2F 11
Marigold Cl. WR5: Worc 4G 21
 WR11: Eves 1G 39
Marion Cl. WR3: Worc 5F 13
Mark Cl. WR14: Mal 1C 26
Market Ga. WR10: Per 5D 34
Market House 3C 42

Market Pas. WR1: Worc 4E 5
Market Pl. WR11: Eves 1D 38
Market St. HR8: Led 3B 42
Market Theatre, The
   Ledbury 3B 42
MARL BANK 3G 31
Marl Bank WR3: Worc 3H 17
Marlbank Rd. WR13: Well . . . . . .5D 30 & 3G 31
   WR14: L Mal .5D 30
Marlborough Gdns. WR14: Mal 1F 27
Marlborough St. WR5: Worc 1A 22
Marlow Cl. WR1: Worc 1C 4
Marlow Rd. WR2: Worc 5B 16
Marsh Av. WR4: Warn 2D 18
Marsh Cl. WR14: Mal 5F 27
Marten Cft. WR5: Worc 4B 22
Martin Av. WR11: Hamp 3A 38
Martin Cl. WR14: Mal 6G 27
Martindale Cl. WR4: Warn 1D 18
Martin's Orchard WR13: C Sto 2A 30
Martins Way HR8: Led 5B 42
Martley Rd. WR2: Worc 2C 16
Maryman's Rd. WR11: Hamp 3B 38
Masefield Av. HR8: Led 1B 42
Masefield Cl. HR8: Led 3B 42
    (off The Homend)
   WR3: Worc 1G 17
Mason Cl. WR14: Mal 4F 27
Masons Ct. WR11: Eves 1F 39
Masons Dr. WR4: Worc 1B 18
Masons Ryde WR10: Per 5D 34
Massey Rd. HR8: Led 2A 42
Masters Cl. WR11: Eves 2E 39
Mathon Rd. WR13: C Sto 1A 30
   WR14: W Mal 6A 26
Matravers Rd. WR14: Mal 5F 27
Matthias Cl. WR14: Mal 2E 27
Maund St. WR2: Worc 5F 17
May Av. WR4: Worc 1H 5 (3A 18)
Maybank WR14: Mal 4G 27
Maycroft WR11: Hamp 3B 38
Mayfair WR11: Eves 3D 38
Mayfield Av. WR3: Worc 2G 17
Mayfield Gro. WR14: Mal 5G 27
Mayfield Rd. WR3: Worc 2H 17
   WR10: Per 3D 34
   WR13: Mad 5G 27
Mayflower Cl. WR14: Mal 1F 29
Mayflower Rd. WR9: D Spa 1E 11
Maytree Hill WR9: D Spa 3E 11
Mead, The WR2: Worc 3C 16
Meade Ct. WR11: Eves 1C 38
    (off Merstow Pl.)
Meadowbank Dr. WR2: Worc 6B 16
Meadow Cl. WR5: Kemp 5G 25
   WR8: Bau 1H 33
   WR9: D Spa 5B 8
Meadow Ct. WR9: D Spa 4B 8
Meadow Grn. WR9: D Spa 4B 8
Meadow Orchard WR12: B'way 5G 41
Meadow Piece WR9: D Spa 4B 8
Meadow Pl. WR9: D Spa 4B 8
Meadow Rd. WR3: Worc 4F 13
   WR9: D Spa 5B 8
   WR14: Mal 4C 27
Meadows, The WR3: Fern H 2A 14
Meadows End WR11: Hamp 2B 38
Meadowsweet Ct. WR14: Mal 2G 29
Meadow Wlk. WR9: D Spa 5B 8
   WR10: Per 3E 35
   WR13: C Sto 1B 30
Meadow Way WR9: D Spa 4B 8
Meadway WR14: Mal 2D 26
Mealcheapen St. WR1: Worc 4E 5 (5G 17)
Medina Ho. WR5: Worc 1G 21
Medway Rd. WR5: Worc 4H 5 (5A 18)
    (not continuous)
   WR11: Eves 3F 39
Melbourne St. WR3: Worc 1F 17
Melrose Cl. WR4: Worc 4D 16
Melsungen Allee WR11: Eves 1D 38
    (off Vine St.)
Mendip Cl. WR4: Warn 3B 18
   WR14: Mal 6F 27
Menston Cl. WR4: Warn 3C 18
Mercia Dr. WR9: Hamp L 2A 8
Merebrook Cl. WR14: Mal W 4F 31
Merick Rd. WR14: Mal 2F 27
Merrick Ho. WR2: Worc 5A 4
Merrievale Ct. WR14: Mal 1F 29
Merriman's Ct. WR3: Worc 2G 17
Merriman's Hill Rd. WR3: Worc 2G 17
Merriman's Wlk. WR3: Worc 2G 17
Merrivale Ho. WR1: Worc 4D 4

Merrybrook WR11: Hamp 1A 38
Merry Brook Hgts. WR11: Hamp 2A 38
Merryfields WR13: Well 4G 31
Mersey Rd. WR5: Worc 5A 18
Merstow Cotts. WR11: Eves 1C 38
Merstow Grn. WR11: Eves 1C 38
Merstow Pl. WR11: Eves 1C 38
Merton Cl. WR4: Worc 4A 18
Merton Rd. WR14: Mal 3E 27
Mews, The HR8: Led 3B 42
    (Long Acres)
   HR8: Led 2B 42
    (Robinson's Mdw.)
Michael Cres. WR14: Mal 1D 26
Michael Tippett Dr. WR4: Worc 4A 18
Middle Hollow Dr. WR4: Warn 2C 18
Middle La. WR9: D Spa, H'zor 3B 8
Middle Rd. WR2: Worc 6A 4 (6D 16)
Middles Av. WR4: Warn 3D 18
Middle St. WR1: Worc 2E 5 (4G 17)
Middleton Gdns. WR4: Warn 2D 18
Midhurst Cl. WR5: Worc 1A 22
Midland Rd. WR5: Worc 3G 5 (4H 17)
Midsummer Cl. WR14: Mal 2B 26
Milestone, The WR10: Per 5D 34
Milestone Rd. WR8: Upt Sev 4A 32
Mill Av. WR12: B'way 6E 41
Mill Bank WR11: Eves 1E 39
Millbrook Cl. WR3: Worc 6E 13
Millennium Way WR11: Eves 5E 39
Miller Craddock Way HR8: Led 5B 42
Millers Cl. WR4: Worc 1B 18
Millers Cft. WR14: Mal 2H 29
Miller St. WR9: D Spa 6D 8
Millhams Av. WR4: Warn 2D 18
Mill Ho. Caravan & Camping Site
   WR3: Clain 1F 13
Mill La. WR8: Upt Sev 2A 32
   WR9: Wych 1E 9
   WR10: Per, W Pid 2D 34
   WR11: Ald 1A 40
   WR11: Bad 3B 40
   WR11: Off 4G 37
   WR13: C Sto 2A 30
   WR14: Mal 3H 29
Mill La. Cl. WR10: Per 2E 35
Mill Rd. WR11: Hamp 3B 38
Mill Row Cotts. WR10: Per 2D 34
Mills Cl. WR12: B'way 5G 41
Mill St. WR1: Worc 6D 4 (6F 17)
   WR11: Eves 1D 38
Mill Wood Dr. WR4: Warn 3D 18
Milret Cl. WR3: Worc 2G 17
Milton Cl. WR3: Worc 1G 17
Milton Ct. WR14: Mal 5E 27
Minett Av. WR2: R'ick 1A 20
Minge La. WR8: Upt Sev 4C 32
Minter Av. WR9: D Spa 1C 10
Moat Cres. WR14: Mal 6H 27
Moat Ho. La. WR3: Hind 4H 13
Moatway WR14: Mal 6H 27
Monarch Dr. WR2: Worc 1C 16
Monarch Pl. WR2: Worc 2C 16
Monks Cl. WR10: Per 5D 34
Monks Wlk. WR11: Eves 1D 38
Monkcwell Ho. WR1: Worc 3D 4
Monnow Cl. WR9: D Spa 3C 10
   WR14: Mal 1H 29
Monsell La. WR8: Upt Sev 5A 32
Montfort St. WR11: Eves 1F 39
Montgomerie Cl. WR2: Pow 1A 24
Montpelier Rd. WR14: W Mal 1A 28
Montreal Cl. WR2: Worc 3D 20
Moor Ho. WR1: Worc 6F 17
    (off Armstrong Dr.)
Moorlands, The WR14: Mal W 2F 31
Moorlands Rd. WR14: Mal 2D 26
Moors, The WR1: Worc 1B 4 (3E 17)
Moor St. WR1: Worc 2C 4 (4F 17)
Moreland Rd. WR9: D Spa 1C 10
Moreton Pl. WR1: Worc 4C 4 (5F 17)
Morgan Ct. WR14: Mal 4D 26
Morgan Motor Company Vis. Cen. 4F 27
Morrin Cl. WR2: B'way 4F 13
Morris Av. WR3: Worc 5F 13
Morris Rd. WR2: B'way 5G 41
Mortimers Quay WR11: Eves 1E 39
Mortlake Av. WR5: Worc 6B 18
Morton Av. WR3: Fern H 3A 14
Morton Rd. WR3: Fern H 3A 14
Mosel Dr. WR9: D Spa 3B 10
Moseley Rd. WR2: Hall 2A 12
Mountbatten Rd. WR14: Mal 5G 27
Mt. Pleasant WR10: Per 3D 34
Mt. Pleasant Barns WR10: Per 3D 34

Mount Rd. WR11: Eves 2F 39
MSJ Sports & Fitness Cen. 6E 27
Mucknell Farm La. WR7: Stoult 6G 23
Mulberry Dr. WR8: Upt Sev 4A 32
   WR14: Mal W 5D 28
Mulberry Ter. WR4: Worc 3A 18
Mulberry Tree Hill WR9: D Spa 3E 11
Muncaster Pl. WR4: Warn 1E 19
Murren Av. WR14: Mal 4E 29
Myatt Rd. WR11: Off 2G 37

N

Nailers Row WR11: Eves 1E 39
    (off Castle St.)
Nailsworth Cl. WR4: Warn 6B 14
NAPLETON 6H 25
Napleton La. WR5: Kemp 5G 25
Narrow Wlk. WR2: Worc 6D 16
   WR5: Whitt 3D 22
Nash Cl. WR3: Worc 4E 13
Nash Ct. WR14: Mal 2A 14
Nash's & Wyatt's Almhouses WR1: Worc . . .4E 5
Nash's Pas. WR1: Worc 4E 5
NAUNTON 5H 33
Navigation Rd. WR5: Worc 2F 21
Neason Cl. WR4: Warn 3D 18
Nelson Rd. WR2: Worc 5A 4 (5D 16)
Nether Grange WR14: Mal 6E 27
Netherton Ct. WR1: Worc 3C 4
Netherton La. WR1: Worc 3C 4 (4F 17)
NETHERWICH 5D 8
Netherwich Gdns. WR9: D Spa 5C 8
Newark Grn. WR4: Worc 1F 19
New Bank St. WR3: Worc 1F 17
NEWBRIDGE GREEN 6B 32
Newbury Pk. HR8: Led 2B 42
Newbury Rd. WR2: Worc 4C 16
Newcastle Cl. WR5: Worc 6B 18
New Chawson La. WR9: D Spa 2A 10
Neweys Hill WR3: Worc 6E 13
NEWLAND 2G 27
NEWLAND COMMON 6E 11
Newland Comn. Rd. WR9: New 5E 11
Newland Cres. WR2: R'ick 1B 20
Newland Dr. WR9: D Spa 2D 10
Newland La. WR9: New 5E 11
Newland Rd. WR9: D Spa 2D 10
   WR9: New 4E 11
Newlands WR10: Per 5C 34
Newmans Pas. WR1: Worc 2D 4
New Mills Ind. Est. HR8: Led 3A 42
New Mills Way HR8: Led 2A 42
Newport Ho. WR1: Worc 4C 4
Newport St. WR1: Worc 4C 4 (5F 17)
New Rd. WR2: Worc 5B 4 (5E 17)
   WR10: Per 5C 34
   WR11: Hamp .2B 38
   WR11: Off 3H 37
New St. HR8: Led .5C 42
   WR1: Worc 4E 5 (5G 17)
   WR8: Upt Sev .3B 32
   WR11: Eves 1E 39
Newton Cl. HR8: Led 5C 42
NEWTOWN 6D 8
Newtown Rd. WR5: Worc 3H 5 (4H 17)
   WR14: Mal 3C 26
Newtown Rd. Trad. Est.
   WR5: Worc 3H 5 (4H 17)
Nibley Cl. WR4: Warn 6B 14
Nightingale Av. WR4: Warn 4E 19
Nightingale Cl. WR9: D Spa 4F 11
Nightingale Ct. WR11: Eves 1D 38
Nightingale Ho. WR5: Worc 4G 5 (5H 17)
Nightingale Pl. WR9: D Spa 4F 11
Nightingale Rd. WR14: Mal 5G 27
Nine Acres Grn. WR4: Warn 3D 18
Nine Foot Way WR5: Worc 6D 8
Ninetynine Steps WR14: Mal 1C 28
Nixon Cl. WR2: C End 3D 24
Noble Vw. WR14: W Mal 4B 26
Nogains WR10: Per 6D 34
Norbury Ho. WR9: D Spa 6D 8
    (off Friar St.)
Norbury Theatre & Cinema 6D 8
Norfolk Cl. WR2: Worc 4A 16
Norham Pl. WR4: Warn 1E 19
Norman Cl. WR4: Warn 1D 18
Northampton La. WR9: Omb 2A 6
North Bank WR9: D Spa 3C 8
Northbank, The WR1: Worc 6F 17
    (off Armstrong Dr.)
Northbrook Cl. WR3: Worc 2F 17
Northcote St. WR3: Worc 1F 17

North Cft. WR2: Worc 1C 20
Northdown Cl. HR8: Led 2A 42
NORTH END 4H 27
North End WR10: Pin 1A 34
North End La. WR13: Mad 4G 27
　WR14: Mal 5F 27
Northfield Cl. WR3: Fern H 2B 14
Northfield La. WR2: C End 4A 24
Northfield St. WR1: Worc 1D 4 (3G 17)
North Hill Gdns. WR14: Mal 4C 26
Northleach Cl. WR4: Warn 5B 14
NORTH MALVERN 4C 26
Nth. Malvern Rd. WR14: Mal 4B 26
Northmead HR8: Led 2B 42
North Pde. WR1: Worc 4C 4 (5F 17)
North Quay WR1: Worc 4C 4 (5F 17)
North Rd. WR11: Eves 1F 39
North St. WR9: D Spa 6C 8
North St. Ind. Est.
　WR9: D Spa 6C 8
Northview Ct. WR14: Mal 2C 26
North Wlk. WR14: Mal 5C 26
NORTHWICK 5E 13
Northwick Av. WR3: Worc 1E 17
Northwick Cl. WR3: Worc 5E 13
Northwick Cl. WR3: Worc 6F 13
Northwick Rd. WR3: Bev, Worc 4E 13
　WR11: Eves 1E 39
Northwick Wlk. WR3: Worc 6E 13
NORTON 6D 22
Norton Cl. WR5: Worc 3G 21
Norton Rd. WR5: Kemp 4A 22
　WR5: Kemp, Worc 4H 21
　WR5: Worc 3H 21
Norval Cres. WR11: Off 2G 37
Norwich Rd. WR5: Worc 5B 18
Nuffield Cl. WR2: Worc 3C 16
Nuffield Dr. WR9: D Spa 6A 8
Nuffield Health Club
　Worcester 6G 13
Nunnery Av. WR9: D Spa 1C 10
Nunnery La. WR5: Worc 6B 18
Nunnery Way WR4: Worc 6E 19
Nunnery Wood (Local Nature Reserve) . . .5D 18
Nunnery Wood Sports Complex 6C 18
Nursery Cl. WR10: Per 4D 34
Nursery Rd. WR2: Worc 1C 20
　WR14: Mal 4C 26
Nursery Wlk. WR2: Worc 1C 20
Nyali Ho. WR5: Worc 6H 17
　　　　　　　　　　　　　　(off Victoria Pl.)

O

Oak Apple Cl. WR3: Fern H 1B 14
Oak Av. WR4: Worc 2A 18
Oak Cl. WR11: Bad 1C 40
Oak Cres. WR14: Mal 6G 27
Oak Dr. WR13: C Sto 1A 30
Oakfield Cl. WR5: Kemp 5H 21
Oakfield Dr. WR5: Kemp 5G 25
Oakfield Rd. WR9: Omb 4A 6
　WR14: Mal 2E 27
Oakham Dr. WR9: D Spa 1A 10
Oakham Grn. WR9: D Spa 1A 10
　　　　　　　　　　　　　　　　(off Little Hill)
Oakham Pl. WR9: D Spa 1B 10
Oakland Av. WR9: D Spa 2C 10
Oakland Cl. WR8: Upt Sev 4A 32
Oakland Dr. HR8: Led 4B 42
Oaklands WR5: Worc 1D 18
　WR14: Mal W 2F 31
Oaklands, The WR9: D Spa 2C 10
Oaklands Ct. WR5: Worc 1H 21
Oakleigh Av. WR2: Hall 3A 12
Oakleigh Heath WR2: Hall 3A 12
Oakleigh Rd. WR9: D Spa 2A 10
Oakley Cl. WR14: Mal 6G 27
Oakmoore Ct. WR9: Hamp L 2A 8
Oakridge Cl. WR14: Mal 1C 18
Oak Row WR8: Upt Sev 4C 32
Oaks, The WR5: Kemp 5G 25
Oak St. WR8: Upt Sev 4C 32
Oak Tree Cl. WR11: Eves 3E 39
Oakville Cl. WR2: Worc 2C 20
Oatfields WR9: D Spa 2B 10
Oatleys Cres. HR8: Led 3A 42
Oatleys Rd. HR8: Led 4B 42
Oatleys Ter. HR8: Led 3B 42
Oat St. WR11: Eves 1D 38
Odeon Cinema
　Worcester 3D 4
OFFENHAM 2G 37
OFFENHAM CROSS 4H 37

Offenham Rd. WR11: Eves 1G 39
Offerton Barns Bus. Cen. WR3: Hind 4G 15
Offerton La. WR3: Hind 5G 15
　WR4: Warn 5E 15
Offley St. WR3: Worc 1F 17
Ogilvy Sq. WR3: Worc 5E 13
O'Key's La. WR3: Fern H 2C 14
Old Bakery, The WR3: B'way 5E 41
Old Baskerville WR1: Worc 2F 17
　　　　　　　　　　　　　(off Barbourne Rd.)
OLDBURY 3A 16
Oldbury Rd. WR1: Lwr Bro, Worc . . .2A 4 (3A 16)
Old Chawson La. WR9: D Spa 2A 10
Old Church Rd. WR13: C Sto 1A 30
Old Coach, The WR12: B'way 5H 41
Old Coach Rd. WR9: D Spa 1C 10
Old Drive, The WR3: Hind 2C 14
OLDFIELD 2A 6
Oldfield La. WR9: Omb 2B 6
OLD HILLS 5B 24
Old Hollow WR14: W Mal, Mal 5A 26
Old Malthouse Ct. WR1: Worc 3F 17
　　　　　　　　　　　　　　(off Brewery Wlk.)
Old Malvern Rd. WR2: Pow 6A 20
Old Market Ct. WR10: Per 4D 34
Old Mill, The WR12: B'way 5F 41
Old Northwick La. WR3: Worc 5D 12
Old Orchard WR8: Upt Sev 4A 32
Old Orchard La. WR13: C Sto 1A 30
Old Post Office La. WR11: Bad 2C 40
Old Rackets Ct., The
　WR1: Worc 2E 5
Old Rectory Cl. WR2: Pow 6C 20
Old Rd. WR2: Worc 3D 20
Old Rd. Nth. WR5: Kemp 4G 25
Old Rd. Sth. WR5: Kemp 6F 25
Old School Cl. WR10: Per 5D 34
　WR11: Off 2G 37
Old School Ct. WR11: Hamp 2B 38
Old School Ho., The WR11: Eves 1F 39
Old St. WR8: Upt Sev 4C 32
Old Vicarage Cl. WR5: Kemp 5G 25
OLD WHARF 5A 42
Old Wharf Ind. Est. HR8: Led 5A 42
Old Wyche Rd. WR14: Mal W 5C 28
OMBERSLEY 4A 6
Ombersley Cl. WR9: D Spa 6C 8
Ombersley Rd. WR3: Worc 1F 17
　WR9: D Spa 6C 8
Ombersley St. E. WR9: D Spa 6D 8
Ombersley St. W. WR9: D Spa 6C 8
Ombersley Way WR9: D Spa 1A 10
Ongrils Cl. WR10: Per 4C 34
Ontario Cl. WR2: Worc 3C 20
Orchard, The WR2: Pow 6A 20
Orchard Av. WR12: B'way 5H 41
Orchard Bus. Pk. HR8: Led 1A 42
Orchard Cl. WR2: Hall 4B 12
　WR2: R'ick 1A 20
　WR8: Rya 3E 33
　WR10: Per 5C 34
Orchard Gro. WR11: Off 3G 37
Orchard La. HR8: Led 3B 42
Orchard Lea WR9: D Spa 2E 11
Orchard Pl. HR8: Led 5C 42
Orchard Ri. HR8: Led 2B 42
　WR9: D Spa 3C 10
Orchard Rd. WR10: Per 5C 34
　WR14: Mal 1D 28
Orchard St. WR5: Worc 2G 21
Orchard Wlk. WR11: Eves 3D 38
Orchard Way WR2: C End 4D 24
Orchid Cl. WR5: Worc 5G 21
Orchid Ct. WR14: Mal 3G 29
Orford Way WR14: Mal 5G 27
Oriel Cl. WR4: Worc 2H 5 (4A 18)
Orleans Cl. WR11: Eves 4D 38
Orleton Cl. WR13: Well 3G 31
Orlham La. HR8: Led, Ledd 6A 42
Orlin Rd. WR13: C Sto 1A 30
Orwin Grn. WR4: Warn 4D 18
Osborne Rd. WR14: Mal 3E 27
Osier Cl. WR5: Worc 2G 21
Osprey Cl. WR2: Worc 3E 21
Ostler Dr. WR2: Worc 4C 16
Otley Cl. WR4: Warn 3C 18
Ottawa Cl. WR2: Worc 2C 20
Otter La. WR5: Worc 3B 22
Overbrook WR11: Eves 2E 39
Overthwart Cres. WR4: Warn 2E 19
Owletts End WR10: Pin 1B 34
　WR11: Eves 2E 39
Owletts La. WR10: Wick 6H 35
Oxford Cl. WR5: Worc 5B 18

Oxford Rd. WR14: Mal 5D 26
Oxford Sq. WR14: Mal 5D 26

P

Packers Hill WR8: Upt Sev 4A 32
Packhorse Cl. WR2: Worc 4C 16
Packington Rd. WR2: Worc 2C 16
　WR9: D Spa 1C 10
Packs Cl. WR11: Bad 1B 40
Paddock, The HR8: Led 4B 42
Paddock Dr. WR9: D Spa 4A 8
　WR10: Per 4C 34
Paddock Grn. WR9: D Spa 4B 8
　　　　　　　　　　　　　　(off Paddock Way)
Paddock Hill WR9: D Spa 4B 8
　　　　　　　　　　　　　　(off Paddock Way)
Paddock Way WR9: D Spa 4B 8
Padgewell Hill WR9: D Spa 1B 10
Padmore St. WR1: Worc 2F 5 (4G 17)
Painswick Cl. WR4: Warn 6C 14
Painted Room, The (Fresco Gallery) 3C 42
　　　　　　　　　　　　　　　(off Church La.)
Palmers Grn. WR2: Worc 6D 16
Paper Mill La. WR9: Wych 1E 9
Park & Ride
　Perdiswell 5G 13
　Sixways 5G 15
Park Av. WR3: Worc 1E 17
Park Blvd. WR2: Worc 2E 21
Park Cl. WR14: Mal 3F 27
Parker Pl. WR12: B'way 5G 41
Parkfield WR14: Mal 6D 26
Parkfield La. WR2: Hall 6B 12
Park Heath WR2: Hall 2B 12
Parkland Rd. WR3: Worc 4E 13
Parklands, The WR2: Pow 6A 20
　WR9: D Spa 2D 10
Parklands Mobile Home Pk. WR11: Hamp . .2B 38
Park La. WR2: Hall 5B 12
　WR3: Worc 1E 17
　WR14: Mal W 3A 28
Park Rd. WR14: W Mal 1A 28
Parks, The WR11: Eves 5G 39
Parkside WR13: C Sto 2B 30
Park St. WR5: Worc 5F 5 (5G 17)
Park Vw. WR14: Mal 1D 28
Park Vw. Ter. WR3: Worc 1E 17
Park Way WR9: D Spa 5B 8
Parsonage La. WR9: Omb 5A 6
Parsonage Way WR4: Warn 2F 19
Parsons Cnr. WR9: D Spa 2B 10
　　　　　　　　　　　　　(off Padgewell Hill)
Partridge Cl. WR5: Worc 4H 21
Partridge Retail Pk. WR9: D Spa 4C 8
Patterdale Dr. WR4: Warn 2C 18
Peabody Av. WR4: Warn 3E 19
Peachfield Cl. WR14: Mal W 4D 28
Peachfield Rd. WR14: Mal W 5C 28
Peachley La. WR2: Hall, Lwr Bro 5A 12
Peacock Cl. WR5: Worc 4A 22
Peak Vw. WR14: Mal 2D 26
Pearmain Cl. WR2: Worc 1C 16
Pear Tree Cl. WR14: Mal W 5C 28
Pear Tree Way WR9: Wych 1E 9
Pearwood Cl. WR11: Hamp 3A 38
Pedlingham Cl. WR13: C Sto 1A 30
Peewit Rd. WR11: Hamp 3A 38
Pegasus Cl. WR12: B'way 5F 41
Pelham Rd. WR9: D Spa 3C 10
Pembroke Pl. WR4: Warn 2F 19
Penbury St. WR3: Worc 6F 13
Pendas Mdw. WR10: Pin 3A 34
Pendragon Cl. WR14: Mal 4G 27
Penelope Gdns. WR11: W'ford 5B 40
Penhill Cres. WR2: Worc 4B 16
Peninsula Rd. WR5: B Vill 5B 22
Penmanor Cl. WR2: Worc 5C 16
Penrice Rd. WR9: D Spa 2C 10
Penrith Cl. WR4: Warn 1D 18
Pensham Hill WR10: Per 6E 35
Pepperpot, The 3C 32
　　　　　　　　　　　　　　　(off Church St.)
Pepperpot M. WR8: Upt Sev 3C 32
Percheron Way WR9: D Spa 3F 11
Perch Rd. WR5: Worc 4G 21
Percy Walton Cl. WR14: Mal 3E 29
Perdiswell (Park & Ride) 5G 13
Perdiswell Leisure Cen. 6H 13
Perdiswell Pk. WR3: Clain 5G 13
Perdiswell Pk. Golf Course 6H 13
Perdiswell St. WR3: Worc 6F 13
Perrins Cl. WR14: Mal 3C 26
Perrins Fld. WR8: Upt Sev 4A 32

Perrins Ho. WR14: Mal 5D **26**
Perrycroft Cl. WR3: Fern H 2B **14**
Perry Wood Cl. WR5: Worc 6A **18**
Perry Wood (Local Nature Reserve) 5A **18**
Perrywood Trad. Pk. WR5: Worc 6H **5** (5A **18**)
Perry Wood Wlk. WR5: Worc 6H **5** (6A **18**)
Perscoran Way WR10: Per 6D **34**
PERSHORE 5D **34**
Pershore Abbey .5D **34**
Pershore Bridge .6E **35**
PERSHORE COMMUNITY HOSPITAL 4D **34**
Pershore Hall WR10: Per 3D **34**
Pershore Heritage Cen. *5D 34*
(within Town Hall, High St.)
Pershore La. WR3: Hind, M Hus, Warn 6A **10**
WR4: Warn 6G **15**
WR5: Spet .3H **19**
Pershore Leisure Cen. 5E **35**
Pershore Mkt. WR10: Per 4D **34**
Pershore Retail Mkt. *WR10: Per* *5D 34*
(off King George Way)
Pershore Rd. WR11: Eves, Hamp 2A **38**
Pershore Station (Rail) 3A **34**
Pershore Ter. WR10: Pin 3A **34**
Pershore Trad. Est. WR10: Per 1E **35**
Peterborough Cl. WR5: Worc 5B **18**
Petersfield Dr. WR9: D Spa 1F **11**
Peterson Ct. WR14: Mal 6D **26**
Petunia Cl. WR5: Worc 4H **21**
Pevensey Cl. WR5: Worc 1A **22**
Pheasant St. WR1: Worc 3F **5** (4G **17**)
Philip Rd. WR3: Worc 4F **13**
Philipscote WR11: Eves 1F **39**
(not continuous)
Phillips Rd. WR12: B'way 4G **41**
Phipps Cl. WR10: W Pid 1G **35**
Phoenix Ct. WR1: Worc 5G **17**
Pickering Grn. WR4: Warn 1E **19**
Pickersleigh Av. WR14: Mal 3F **27**
Pickersleigh Cl. WR14: Mal 3F **27**
Pickersleigh Gro. WR14: Mal 4E **27**
Pickersleigh M. WR14: Mal 4E **27**
Pickersleigh Rd. WR14: Mal 4E **27**
Picton Garden (Old Court Nurseries) 6A **28**
Pierpoint Ct. WR1: Worc 2D **4**
Pierpoint St. WR1: Worc 2D **4** (4F **17**)
Piers Cl. WR14: Mal 4E **29**
Pike Cl. WR5: Worc 4G **21**
Pike Cnr. WR12: Will 1H **41**
Pilgrim Rd. WR9: D Spa 1F **11**
Pinder Hgts. *WR11: Eves* *1E 39*
(off Conduit Hill)
Pine Cl. WR3: Fern H 2C **14**
Pine Way WR4: Worc 1A **18**
Pinewood Ho. *WR3: Worc* *6F 13*
(off Coombs Rd.)
Pinkett St. WR3: Worc 6E **13**
Pinkus Cl. WR4: Warn 4E **19**
Pinnacle Way WR14: Mal 2C **26**
PINVIN 2A **34**
Pippen Fld. WR4: Warn 2E **19**
Pippin Cl. WR10: Per 3D **34**
Pippin Cl. WR11: Hamp 3A **38**
Pirie Av. WR4: Worc 4E **19**
PITCHCROFT 1A **4** (3E **17**)
Pitchcroft La. WR1: Worc 2E **17**
Pitchers Hill WR11: W'ford 6A **40**
Pitmaston Rd. WR2: Worc 6D **16**
Pitmaston Wlk. WR2: Worc 1D **20**
Pitt Av. WR4: Warn 4D **18**
Pitwell La. WR11: Ald 5H **37**
Pixham 5E **25**
Pixham Ferry La. WR2: C End 5C **24**
WR5: Kemp 6F **25**
Pixie Path, The WR14: Mal W 5B **28**
Plaister's End HR8: Led 1B **42**
Plantation Dr. WR4: Warn 2D **18**
Players Av. WR14: Mal 2E **27**
Plaza WR1: Worc 5G **17**
Plough Cft. WR4: Warn 2D **18**
Ploughmans Cl. WR4: Worc 1B **18**
Ploughmans Cl. WR9: D Spa 4B **8**
Ploughmans Piece *WR9: D Spa* *4B 8*
(off Ploughmans Way)
Ploughmans Ri. WR9: D Spa 4B **8**
Ploughmans Wlk. WR9: D Spa 4B **8**
Ploughmans Way WR9: D Spa 4B **8**
Plough Yd. *HR8: Led* *3B 42*
(off The Homend)
Plovers Ri. WR5: Kemp 5G **25**
Pointon Way WR9: Hamp L 2H **7**
POLE ELM 3D **24**
Pole Elm Cl. WR2: C End 3D **24**
Pollard Ct. *WR5: Worc* *1G 21*
(off Layland Wlk.)

Pool, The WR11: Hamp 2B **38**
(off Old School Ct.)
POOLBROOK 3G **29**
Poolbrook Rd. WR14: Mal 4F **29**
Pool Orchard WR12: Will 2H **41**
Pope Iron Rd. WR1: Worc 2E **17**
Poplar Av. WR4: Worc 2A **18**
WR10: W Pid 1G **35**
Poplar Cl. HR8: Led 2A **42**
WR11: Eves 3F **39**
Poplar Ct. WR11: Bad 2C **40**
Poplars, The *WR9: Wych* *2E 9*
(off Worcester Rd.)
WR11: Bad 2B **40**
Poppy Cl. WR11: Eves 1G **39**
Portefields Rd. WR4: Worc 3B **18**
Porter Rd. WR11: Eves 2F **39**
Port Ho. WR1: Worc 2F **5**
Portland Point *WR1: Worc* *6F 17*
(off Armstrong Dr.)
Portland Rd. WR9: D Spa 2F **11**
WR14: Mal 6D **26**
Portland St. WR1: Worc 6F **17**
Portland Wlk. WR1: Worc 6F **17**
Portsmouth Cl. WR5: Worc 5B **18**
Port St. WR11: Eves 1E **39**
Post Office La. WR3: Fern H 2C **14**
WR5: Kemp 4G **25**
Potters Cl. WR4: Worc 1B **18**
POUND BANK 1G **29**
Pound Bank Rd.
WR14: Mal 1G **29**
Pound Cl. HR8: Led 4C **42**
Pound Comn. WR14: Mal 1G **29**
Pound Mdw. HR8: Led 4B **42**
Pound Wlk. WR1: Worc 2E **17**
Powderham Av. WR4: Warn 1E **19**
Powell's Row WR2: Worc 6A **4** (6E **17**)
POWICK 1A **24**
POWICK VILLAGE 5C **20**
Powick Wlk. WR1: Worc 4D **4**
Powyke Ct. Cl. WR2: Pow 6B **20**
Preece Cl. WR14: Mal 1D **26**
Prescott Dr. WR4: Warn 5C **14**
Prestbury Cl. WR4: Warn 6B **14**
Preston Brook Cl. HR8: Led 2B **42**
Preston St. *WR3: Fern H* *2A 14*
(off Eastfield Cl.)
Prestwich Av. WR5: Worc 6B **18**
Price's La. WR8: Upt Sev 4C **32**
Price St. WR3: Worc 1F **17**
Pridzor Ct. WR9: D Spa 5E **9**
Pridzor Rd. WR9: D Spa 5E **9**
Priest La. WR10: Per 4D **34**
Primrose Cl. WR14: Mal 2G **29**
Primrose Cres. WR5: Worc 4H **21**
Primrose Dr. WR5: Worc 4H **21**
PRIMSLAND 3E **11**
Primsland Dr. WR9: D Spa 2F **11**
Primsland Flds. WR9: D Spa 3E **11**
Primsland Way WR9: D Spa 3C **10**
Prince Edward's Cl.
WR11: Eves 4E **37**
Prince Henry's Cl. WR11: Eves 4E **37**
Prince Rupert Av. WR2: Pow 1A **24**
Prince Rupert Rd. HR8: Led 5F **5** (5G **17**)
WR5: Worc 5F **5** (5G **17**)
Princes Av. WR9: D Spa 2D **10**
Princes Dr. WR1: Worc 6E **5** (6G **17**)
Princess Margaret Av.
WR14: Mal 2G **27**
Princess Rd. WR11: Eves 5E **37**
Priors Wlk. WR10: Per 5D **34**
WR11: Eves 2E **39**
Priory Ct. WR14: Mal 1D **28**
Priory Gdns. WR9: D Spa 6D **8**
Priory La. WR9: D Spa 6D **8**
Priory Rd. WR2: Worc 1D **20**
WR14: Mal 1D **28**
Priory Wlk. *WR1: Worc* *3F 17*
(off Lansdowne Rd.)
Progress Cl. HR8: Led 1A **42**
Prospect Cl. WR14: Mal 0F **27**
Prospect Cl. WR11: Eves 1G **39**
Prospect Gdns. WR11: Eves 1F **39**
Prospect Pl. WR5: Worc 6F **5** (6G **17**)
Prospect Vw. WR14: Mal 6F **27**
Providence St. WR1: Worc 4F **5** (5G **17**)
Pry La. WR12: B'way 6E **41**
Pryors Grn. WR11: Bad 2B **40**
Pryors St. WR11: B'way 5G **41**
Pulley La. WR9: Cop, New 4B **10**
Pump House Environment Centre, The 1E **17**
Pump St. WR1: Worc 5E **5** (5G **17**)
WR14: Mal 4C **26**
Purleigh Av. WR4: Warn 2E **19**

Purlieu, The WR14: W Mal 4A **28**
Pyndar Ct. WR13: New 2H **27**

Q

Quabbs, The WR14: W Mal 1A **28**
Quadrangle, The WR13: New 2G **27**
Quay Ho. WR1: Worc 2F **5**
Quay La. WR8: Han C 1A **32**
Quay St. WR1: Worc 4C **4** (5F **17**)
Quebec Cl. WR4: Worc 3C **20**
Queen Elizabeth Dr. WR10: Per 4D **34**
Queen Elizabeth Rd. WR14: Mal 2F **27**
Queen Elizabeths Almshouses *WR1: Worc* . .*3F 17*
(off Upper Tything)
Queen's Cl. WR14: Mal 3C **26**
Queen's Ct. HR8: Led 3B **42**
Queens Ct. M. HR8: Led 3B **42**
Queen's Dr. WR14: Mal 6C **26**
Queens Mead WR8: Upt Sev 5C **32**
Queen's Rd. WR11: Eves 6D **36**
WR14: Mal 6D **26**
Queen St. WR1: Worc 3E **5** (4G **17**)
WR9: D Spa 6E **9**
Queens Wlk. HR8: Led 3B **42**
Queenswood Dr. WR5: Worc 4H **21**
Quest Hills Rd. WR14: Mal 3D **26**
Quinary, The WR12: Will 1H **41**
Quisters WR4: Warn 2D **18**

R

Racecourse Rd. WR10: Per 1E **35**
Race Fld. WR4: Warn 2D **18**
Rack All. WR1: Worc 3C **4**
Racks La. WR9: Omb 4B **6**
Radnor Cft. WR3: Worc 6A **14**
Raglan St. WR3: Worc 1F **17**
Rail Ground WR10: Per 4C **34**
Railway Wlk. WR3: Worc 1G **5** (4H **17**)
Rainbow Ct. WR3: Worc 1G **5**
RAINBOW HILL 3H **17**
Rainbow Hill WR3: Worc 2F **5** (4G **17**)
Rainbow Hill Ter. WR3: Worc 1G **5** (3H **17**)
Rainbow Ri. WR3: Worc 3H **17**
Rainthorpe Av. WR5: Worc 3A **22**
Raleigh Cl. WR3: Worc 5B **16**
Ramillies Dr. WR5: B Vill 5B **22**
Ramsons Cl. WR14: Mal 4G **27**
Randwick Cl. WR4: Warn 1B **18**
Randwick Dr. WR4: Warn 6B **14**
Ranelagh Rd. WR14: Mal 2G **27**
Rannoch Av. WR5: Worc 3A **22**
Ransom Av. WR5: Worc 1C **22**
RASHWOOD 2G **9**
Rashwood Hill WR9: Rash 3G **9**
Raven Dr. WR5: Worc 4H **21**
Ravenmeadow Golf Course 4H **13**
Ravenscroft Dr. WR9: D Spa 1F **11**
Ravenshill Cl. WR5: Worc 4A **22**
Rea Way WR2: Worc 5B **16**
Rebekah Gdns. WR9: D Spa 3D **10**
Rectory Gdns. WR2: Worc 4A **4** (5E **17**)
Rectory Ho. WR8: Upt Sev 5D **32**
Rectory La. WR13: Mad 4H **27**
Rectory Pl. WR5: Worc 6F **5**
Rectory Rd. WR8: Upt Sev 4C **32**
Redcliffe St. WR3: Worc 6E **13**
Redfern La. WR14: Mal 1H **29**
Redfern Av. WR5: Worc 6B **18**
RED HILL 1A **22**
Red Hill La. WR5: Worc 2B **22**
WR7: Worc 2B **22**
Redland Cl. WR14: Mal 3E **27**
Redland Rd. WR14: Mal 3E **27**
Redlands WR10: Per 4D **34**
Red La. WR11: Hamp 6B **36**
Redwing Cl. WR14: Mal 1B **26**
Redwood Cl. WR4: Worc 1A **18**
Reed Cl. WR14: Mal 6F **27**
Reedham Cl. WR3: Worc 6E **13**
Regal Cinema
Evesham .1E **39**
Regency Rd. WR14: Mal 2F **27**
Regiment Cl. WR5: B Vill 5B **22**
Regina Cl. WR9: D Spa 3D **10**
Reindeer Ct. Shop. Cen.
WR1: Worc 4E **5** (5G **17**)
Reservoir La. WR3: Worc 1G **5** (3H **17**)
Restdale Ho. WR1: Worc 2D **4**
Retreat, The WR12: B'way 5G **41**
Reynolds Cl. WR13: Well 3G **31**

Rhydd Cl. WR14: Mal 2G 29
Ribble Cl. WR5: Worc 5A 18
Ribston Cl. WR2: Worc 2C 16
Richard's Cl. WR14: Mal 2C 26
Richardson Cl. WR9: Wych 3C 10
Richmond Hill WR5: Worc 5G 5 (5H 17)
Richmond Rd. WR5: Worc 5G 5 (5H 17)
WR14: Mal 3F 27
Richmonds Pitch WR14: Mal W 4E 31
Rickett's La. WR9: D Spa 6D 8
Ridgeway WR13: C Sto 6B 30
Ridgeway, The WR5: Worc 2A 22
WR9: D Spa 1F 11
Rightons Ct. WR11: Eves 6D 36
Ripley Gdns. WR4: Warn 1F 19
Ripon Rd. WR5: Worc 4C 18
Ripple Rd. WR9: D Spa 1C 10
River Ho. WR11: Eves 6E 37
Rivermead Holiday Home Pk.
WR10: W Pid 2F 35
Riverside Cen. WR11: Eves 1D 38
Riverside Cl. WR8: Upt Sev 3C 32
Riverside Rd. WR9: D Spa 6E 9
Riverside Way WR9: D Spa 6F 9
Riverview Cl. WR2: Worc 1C 16
Roach Cl. WR5: Worc 4G 21
Robert Owen Ct. WR1: Worc 4F 5
Robeson Cl. WR9: D Spa 6F 9
Robin Cl. WR5: Worc 4H 21
Robin Dr. WR3: Clain 2A 14
Robinia Cl. WR11: Eves 5D 38
Robins Cnr. WR11: Eves 6E 37
Robins Mdw. WR11: Eves 6E 37
Robinson's Mdw. HR8: Led 2B 42
Robin's Wlk. WR11: Eves 6E 37
Rockingham La. WR4: Warn 1F 19
Rodborough Cl. WR4: Warn 6C 14
Rodborough Dr. WR4: Warn 6C 14
Rogers Hill WR3: Worc 3G 15
Roland Rutter Ct. WR10: Per 4C 34
Roman Way WR9: D Spa 1A 10
WR14: Mal 2G 27
Roman Way Bus. Cen. WR9: D Spa 4C 8
Rona Gdns. WR5: Worc 3B 22
RONKSWOOD 5C 18
Ronkswood Cres. WR5: Worc 4A 18
Ronkswood Hill WR4: Worc 4A 18
Rookery Rd. WR5: Kemp 4G 25
Rose Av. WR4: Worc 1H 5 (3A 18)
WR5: Worc 6G 5 (6H 17)
WR9: D Spa 6F 9
Rose Bank WR3: Clain 3H 13
WR5: Worc 6H 5 (6H 17)
WR11: Eves 1F 39
Rose Cl. WR9: D Spa 6F 9
Rose Hill WR5: Worc 6G 5 (6H 17)
Rosemary Av. WR2: Worc 6B 16
Rosemary Cl. WR11: Hamp 3B 38
Rosemoor Gdns. WR5: Worc 3A 22
Rose Ter. WR5: Worc 6G 5 (6H 17)
Rosewood Cl. WR3: Fern H 3B 14
Rossendale Cl. WR3: Fern H 2B 14
Ross Rd. HR8: Led 5A 42
Rothwell Rd. WR14: Mal W 2F 31
Rough Mdw. WR4: Warn 2D 18
Rowan Av. WR4: Worc 2C 18
Rowan Cl. WR9: D Spa 3D 10
WR11: Eves 5D 38
Rowan Ct. WR4: Worc 3A 18
WR9: D Spa 6D 8
Rowlands Ct. WR11: Eves 1D 38
Rowlands Ho. WR2: Worc 5A 4
Rowley Hill St. WR2: Worc 5D 16
Rowntree Gdns. WR4: Warn 5E 19
Royal Albert Cl. WR5: Worc 6F 5
Royal Arc. WR10: Per 5D 34
Royal Ct. WR5: Worc 6F 5 (6G 17)
Royal Oak Gdns. WR14: Mal 2F 27
Rudd Cl. WR5: Worc 4G 21
Rudge Rd. WR11: Eves 6D 36
Rushdon Ct. WR1: Worc 5E 5
Rusher's Cl. WR10: Per 4C 34
RUSHWICK 1A 20
Rushy Cl. WR9: D Spa 1C 10
Russell Cl. WR2: Pow 1A 24
WR14: Mal 4F 27
Russell Dr. WR14: Mal 3F 27
Russell Ho. WR2: Worc 5A 4
Russell Sq. WR12: B'way 5G 41
Russet Cl. HR8: Led 5B 42
Russett Cl. WR2: Worc 2C 16
Rutland Pl. WR5: Worc 3A 22
Ruyhalls Pl. WR10: Wick 6F 35
RYALL 3E 33
Ryall Ct. La. WR8: Holl G 1D 32

Ryall Gro. WR8: Rya 3F 33
Ryall La. WR8: Rya 4E 33
Ryall Mdw. WR8: Rya 4E 33
Ryall Rd. WR8: Holl G, Rya 3E 33
Rydal Cl. WR4: Warn 2B 18
(not continuous)
Ryden La. WR10: Char 3A 36
Rye Cl. WR9: D Spa 1E 11
Ryeland Cl. WR3: Worc 6A 14
Ryelands WR10: W Pid 1G 35
Rye Lea, The WR9: D Spa 1B 10
(off Padgewell Hill)
Rye Pl. WR4: Warn 1F 19
Rynal Pl. WR11: Eves 6D 36
Rynal St. WR11: Eves 6D 36

S

Sabrina Av. WR3: Worc 1E 17
Sabrina Ter. WR1: Worc 2E 17
Sabrina Wlk. WR3: Worc 6E 13
Sacred Heart Church 2C 10
Saddlers Wlk. WR4: Worc 1B 18
St Agatha's Cl. WR10: Per 4D 34
St Agatha's Ct. WR10: Per 4D 34
St Agathas Rd. WR10: Per 4D 34
St Albans Cl. WR5: Worc 4B 18
St Andrew Rd. WR11: Hamp 2A 38
St Andrew's Cl. WR9: D Spa 6D 8
St Andrew's Ct. WR14: Mal 3E 29
St Andrew's Dr. WR9: D Spa 1D 10
St Andrew's Rd. WR9: D Spa 6D 8
WR10: Per 6C 34
WR14: Mal 4E 29
St Andrew's Spire 4D 4 (5F 17)
St Andrews Sq. WR9: D Spa 6D 8
(within Salters Shop. Cen.)
St Andrew's St. WR9: D Spa 6D 8
St Anne's Cl. WR3: Worc 4G 13
St Anne's Rd. WR3: Worc 4F 13
St Ann's Rd. WR14: Mal 1C 28
St Audrie's Rd. WR5: Worc 1G 21
St Augustine Dr. WR9: D Spa 5E 9
St Augustine's Cl. WR9: D Spa 5E 9
St Bernard Dr. WR14: Mal 4E 29
St Catherine's Hill
WR5: Worc 6H 5 (6H 17)
St Catherines Rd. WR11: Eves 4D 38
St Catherine's Va. WR11: Eves 6A 18
St Christopher Ct. WR11: Eves 5D 36
St Clement's Cl. WR2: Worc 5A 4 (5E 17)
St Clement's Ct. WR2: Worc 4A 4 (5E 17)
St Clement's Gdns. WR2: Worc 5A 4 (5E 17)
St Davids Dr. WR11: Eves 4D 38
St Dunstan's Cl. WR5: Worc 1G 21
St Dunstan's Cres. WR5: Worc 6G 17
St Egwine Cl. WR3: Worc 2G 17
St Egwin's Rd. WR11: Eves 6D 36
St George Cl. HR8: Led 3B 42
St Georges Cl. WR11: Eves 4E 39
St George's Cres. WR9: D Spa 6E 9
St George's La. Nth. WR1: Worc 2F 17
St George's La. Sth. WR1: Worc 2F 17
St George's Sq. WR1: Worc 2F 17
WR9: D Spa 6E 9
St George's Wlk. WR1: Worc 2F 17
St James Cl. WR1: Bad 2C 40
St James' Cres. WR14: W Mal 5A 26
St James Dr. WR11: Eves 4D 38
WR14: Mal 5D 26
St Jamoo'a Rd. WR14: W Mal 5A 26
ST JOHN'S 6A 4 (5E 17)
St John's WR2: Worc 5A 4 (5E 17)
(Bull Ring)
WR2: Worc 6A 4 (6D 16)
(Swanpool Wlk.)
St Johns Cl. WR3: Worc 4F 13
WR11: Eves 4E 39
St John's M. WR2: Worc 6A 4
St John's Sports Cen. 6A 4 (6E 17)
St Joseph's Cl. WR9: D Spa 1B 10
St Katherine's HR8: Led 3C 42
(off High St.)
St Kitts Cl. WR14: Mal 2D 26
St Lawrence Cl. WR2: Worc 2D 20
St Lawrence Rd. WR11: Eves 1C 38
St Lukes Cl. WR11: Eves 4D 38
St Margarets Rd. WR11: Eves 4D 38
St Marks Cl. WR5: Worc 2G 21
WR11: Eves 4D 38
St Marks St. WR5: Worc 2G 21
St Martin's Ga. WR1: Worc 4F 5 (5G 17)
St Mary's Cl. WR5: Kemp 4F 25
St Mary's Ct. WR1: Worc 1D 4

St Mary's Rd. WR9: D Spa 1D 10
WR11: Eves 6D 36
St Mary's St. WR1: Worc 2D 4 (4F 17)
St Matthews Cl. WR11: Eves 4E 39
St Michaels HR8: Led 3C 42
St Michaels Cl. WR11: Eves 5D 38
St Michael's Rd. WR3: Worc 5F 13
St Milburgh Cl. WR11: Off 2G 37
St Moritz Cl. WR3: Worc 5D 12
St Nicholas Ho. WR14: Mal 4C 26
St Nicholas La. WR4: Warn 1F 19
St Nicholas St. WR1: Worc 3D 4 (4G 17)
WR9: D Spa 6C 8
St Oswald's Cl. WR1: Worc 1D 4 (3F 17)
St Oswald's Rd. WR1: Worc 1D 4 (3F 17)
St Patricks Cl. WR11: Eves 4D 38
St Pauls Cl. WR11: Eves 5E 39
St Paul's Ct. WR1: Worc 4F 5
St Paul's St. WR1: Worc 4F 5 (5G 17)
St Peter's Chu. La. WR9: D Spa 1E 11
St Peters Cl. WR11: Eves 2E 39
WR14: Mal W 4F 31
St Peter's Cres. WR9: D Spa 1E 11
St Peter's Dr. WR5: Worc 4H 21
St Peter's Gdns. WR9: D Spa 6E 9
(off St Peter's Wlk.)
St Peter's Hill WR5: Worc 4G 21
St Peter's Rd. WR9: D Spa 1D 10
WR14: Mal 3B 26
St Peters St. WR1: Worc 6E 5 (6G 17)
St Peter's Wlk. WR9: D Spa 6E 9
ST PETER THE GREAT 3A 22
St Philips Dr. WR11: Eves 5D 38
St Richards Cl. WR9: Wych 2E 9
St Richard's Gdns. WR9: D Spa 6C 8
ST RICHARD'S HOSPICE 6D 18
St Richards Rd. WR9: Wych 2E 9
WR11: Eves 4D 38
St Stephens Cl. WR13: C Grn 4A 30
St Stephen's St. WR3: Worc 1F 17
St Stephen's Ter. WR3: Worc 1F 17
St Swithin's St. WR1: Worc 4E 5 (5G 17)
St Swithuns Cl. WR5: Worc 1H 21
St Wulstans Cl. WR11: Eves 4E 39
St Wulstans Cl. WR5: Worc 6E 5
St Wulstan's Cres. WR5: Worc 6G 5 (6H 17)
St Wulstans Dr. WR14: Mal W 4F 31
Salamanca Dr. WR5: B Vill 5B 22
Salisbury Cl. WR11: Eves 5B 18
Salisbury Dr. WR11: Eves 3C 38
Sally Cl. WR11: W'ford 6B 40
Saltbarrow Mkt. WR9: D Spa 6D 8
(off High St.)
Salters Cl. WR4: Worc 1A 18
Salters Ct. WR11: H'zor 1H 11
Salters Shop. Cen. WR9: D Spa 6D 8
Saltway WR9: D Spa 6D 8
Saltwood Av. WR4: Warn 1E 19
Salubrious WR12: B'way 5H 41
Salwarpe Dr. WR9: Wych 2E 9
Salwarpe Rd. WR9: D Spa 6C 8
Sanctuary WR2: Worc 5C 16
Sandles Cl. WR9: D Spa 4D 10
Sandles Rd. WR9: D Spa 4D 10
Sandown Rd. WR11: Eves 3C 38
Sandpiper Cl. WR5: Worc 3A 22
Sandpiper Cres. WR14: Mal 1B 26
Sandringham Cl. WR11: Eves 5D 36
WR14: Mal 1G 27
Sands, The WR12: B'way 5G 41
Sands Cl. WR12: B'way 4G 41
Sandscroft Av. WR12: B'way 4H 41
Sands La. WR11: Bad 3C 40
Sandwell Ho. WR1: Worc 2D 4
Sandys Av. WR11: W'ford 6B 40
Sandys Rd. WR1: Worc 2E 17
WR9: Omb 4A 6
WR14: Mal 4G 27
Sansome Cl. WR11: Eves 3E 5
Sansome Flds. Ho. WR1: Worc 1E 5
Sansome Flds. Wlk.
WR1: Worc 1D 4 (3F 17)
Sansome M. WR1: Worc 1D 4
Sansome Pl. WR1: Worc 3E 5 (4G 17)
Sansome St. WR1: Worc 3D 4 (4G 17)
Sansome Wlk. WR1: Worc 1D 4 (3F 17)
Santler Ct. WR14: Mal 3E 27
Sapphire Cres. WR1: Worc 4C 16
Sarai Cl. WR9: D Spa 4D 10
Saunders St. WR1: Worc 6E 13
Sawmill Cl. WR5: Worc 6H 5 (6A 18)
Saxonbury WR11: Eves 3E 39
SAXON'S LODE .6E 33
Saxon Way HR8: Led 1A 42
Sayers Av. WR14: Mal 3C 26

Scafell Cl. WR4: Warn	Showell Rd. WR9: D Spa	Spring Bank WR3: Hind
Scattergood's Yd. HR8: Led	Shrawley Rd. WR3: Fern H	WR14: Mal
Scholars Wlk. WR9: D Spa	Shrubbery Av. WR1: Worc	Spring Cl. WR13: C Sto
School Bank WR3: Clain	Shrubbery Rd. WR1: Worc	Springfield Cl. WR5: Worc
WR9: Omb	Shrub Hill WR4: Worc	Springfield Dr. WR11: Eves
School Cl. WR10: Pin	Shrub Hill Ind. Est. WR4: Worc	Springfield Glade WR14: Mal
School La. WR8: Upt Sev	Shrub Hill Retail Pk.	Springfield La. WR12: B'way
WR10: Wick	WR5: Worc	Springfield Retail Pk. WR11: Eves
WR11: Bad	Shrub Hill Rd. WR4: Worc	Springfield Rd. WR5: Worc
School Rd. WR2: Worc	Shuttlefast La. WR14: Mal W	Spring Gdns. WR1: Worc
WR9: Wych	Sidbury WR1: Worc	Spring Gro. HR8: Led
WR11: Hamp	Sidbury Ho. WR1: Worc	Spring Hill WR5: Worc
School Wlk. WR5: Whitt	Sidings La. WR11: Ald	Spring La. WR5: Worc
Scobell Cl. WR10: Per	Silverdale Av. WR5: Worc	WR14: Mal
Scotlands, The WR9: D Spa	Silver St. WR1: Worc	Spring La. Ind. Est. WR14: Mal
Seaborne Leisure & Country Homes	WR13: C Sto	Spring La. Nth. WR14: Mal
WR5: Kemp	Simon De Montfort Dr. WR11: Eves	Spring La. Sth. WR14: Mal
Sebright Av. WR5: Worc	Simon's Way WR11: Eves	Spring Mdw. WR4: Warn
Sebright Rd. WR10: Per	Sinclair Ct. WR11: Eves	Square, The WR2: Worc
Sedge Cl. WR2: Worc	Singer Hill WR9: D Spa	Squires, The WR11: Eves
Selborne Rd. WR1: Worc	(off Bower Hill)	Squire's Cft. WR5: Kemp
Selborne Rd. W. WR1: Worc	Sinton La. WR9: Omb	Squire's Wlk. WR5: Kemp
Selsey Cl. WR4: Warn	(not continuous)	Squirrel Dr. WR5: Worc
Seven Acres WR4: Warn	Sinton Ter. WR2: Worc	Stable Ct. WR9: H'zor
Severn Ct. WR9: D Spa	Six Acres Cft. WR4: Warn	Stables, The WR3: Bev
Severndale WR9: D Spa	Sixways	Stafford Av. WR4: Warn
Severn Dr. WR8: Upt Sev	Sixways (Park & Ride)	Stainburn Av. WR2: Worc
WR14: Mal	Six Ways Ind. Est. WR14: Mal	Stainburn Cl. WR2: Worc
Severn Grange WR3: Bev	Skenfrith Pl. WR4: Warn	Stallard Rd. WR2: Worc
Severn Ho. WR2: Worc	Skiddaw Cl. WR4: Warn	Stalls Farm Rd. WR9: D Spa
Severn Motor Yacht Club	Skinner Rd. WR2: Worc	Stanage Cl. WR4: Warn
Severn St. WR1: Worc	Skinner St. WR2: Worc	STANBROOK
Severn Ter. WR1: Worc	Skippe Cl. HR8: Led	Stanbrook Ho. Rd. WR2: C End
Seward Cl. WR11: Bad	Skipton Cres. WR4: Warn	Stanhope Ct. WR2: Worc
WR11: Eves	Sky Ct. WR3: Worc	Stanier Rd. WR4: Warn
Seward Rd. WR11: Bad	Skylark Ri. WR14: Mal	Stanley Rd. WR5: Worc
Seymour Av. WR3: Worc	Skyrrold Rd. WR14: Mal	WR14: Mal
Seymour Ct. WR14: Mal	Slade Av. WR4: Warn	Stanley St. WR5: Worc
Shaftesbury Grn. WR4: Warn	Slimbridge Cl. WR5: Worc	Stanmore Rd. WR2: Worc
Shakespeare Rd. WR2: Worc	Sling La. WR3: Fern H, Hind	Stanway Cl. WR4: Warn
Shambles, The WR1: Worc	WR14: Mal	Stanway Rd. WR5: Worc
Shannon Way WR11: Eves	Slingpool Wlk. WR2: Worc	Star La. WR2: Worc
Shap Dr. WR4: Warn	Smallbrook Rd. WR12: B'way	Starling Cl. WR5: Worc
Sharman Cl. WR1: Worc	Smite Caravan Site WR3: Hind	Station App. WR14: Mal
Sharman Rd. WR1: Worc	SMITE HILL	Station Dr. WR13: C Sto
Sharpe Rd. WR2: Worc	Smite La. WR3: Hind	Station Rd. WR3: Fern H
Shawcross Wlk. WR11: Eves	Smith Ct. WR5: Worc	WR10: Per
Shaw La. WR9: Wych	Smiths Av. WR2: Worc	WR11: B'ter, Off
Shaw St. WR1: Worc	Smiths Way WR10: Per	WR12: B'way
Shaw Wlk. WR14: Mal	Smoke All. HR8: Led	Station Rd. Ind. Est. WR8: Upt Sev
Shear Ho. WR12: B'way	Snowberry Av. WR4: Warn	Station St. WR9: D Spa
Sheepscombe Dr. WR4: Warn	Snowshill Cl. WR4: Warn	Station Wlk. WR4: Worc
Sheffield Cl. WR5: Worc	Snowshill Rd. WR12: B'way	Station Yd. Ind. Est. WR13: C Sto
Shelburne Ter. WR14: Mal	Solent Pl. WR11: Eves	Steamer Point WR14: Mal
Sheldon Av. WR12: B'way	Solent Rd. WR5: Worc	Stephenson Rd. WR1: Worc
Sheldon Cl. WR9: Wych	Solitaire Rd. WR2: Worc	Stephenson Ter. WR1: Worc
WR10: Per	Somers Ct. WR14: Mal	Steynors Av. WR9: D Spa
Sheldon Pk. Rd. WR3: Worc	Somerset Pl. WR1: Worc	Steynors Cl. WR9: D Spa
Shelley Cl. WR3: Worc	Somers Pk. Av. WR14: Mal	Steynors Way WR9: D Spa
Shelsley Dr. WR13: Upp C	Somers Rd. WR14: Mal	Stinton Ct. WR1: Worc
Shenstone Cl. WR14: Mal	WR14: Mal	Stirling Av. WR4: Warn
Shepherds Cl. HR8: Led	Somerville Rd. WR4: Worc	Stock Coppice Cl. WR4: Warn
WR9: D Spa	Sorrel Cl. WR3: Clain	Stoke Rd. WR9: Wych
Shepherds Ct. WR9: D Spa	Sorrel Way WR4: Warn	Stokesay La. WR4: Warn
(off Shepherds Hill)	Southall Av. WR5: Worc	Stonebridge Cross Bus. Pk. WR9: Hamp L
Shepherds Grn. WR9: D Spa	SOUTH BANK SPIRE HOSPITAL	Stone Cl. WR13: C Sto
Shepherds Hill WR9: D Spa	South Cft. WR2: Worc	Ctono Cl. WR13: C Sto
Shepherds Pl. WR9: D Spa	Southdown Rd. WR3: Worc	Stone Dr. WR13: C Sto
Shepherds Pool WR11: Eves	Southend, The HR8: Led	Stoneleigh Cl. WR5: Worc
Shepherds Ri. WR9: D Spa	Southend M. HR8: Led	Stone Pippin Orchard WR11: Bad
(off Shepherds Cl.)	(off The Southend)	Stonewell Ter. WR10: Per
Shepherds Way WR9: D Spa	Southfield St. WR1: Worc	Stoneycroft Cl. WR3: Fern H
Sheridan Row WR4: Warn	South Lawn WR14: Mal W	Stony Cl. WR4: Warn
Sheringham Rd. WR5: Worc	South Pde. HR8: Led	Storer Ct. WR14: Mal
SHERNAL GREEN	WR1: Worc	Stotfield Av. WR4: Warn
SHERRARD'S GREEN	South Pk. Dr. WR9: D Spa	Stouton Cft. WR9: D Spa
Sherrard's Grn. Rd. WR14: Mal	South Quay WR1: Worc	Stowe Cl. WR13: C Sto
Sherriff St. WR4: Worc	South St. WR1: Worc	Strand La. WR3: M Hus
Sherriff St. Commercial Complex	South Vw. WR0: W Pid	STRATFORD
WR4: Worc	Southwold Cl. WR5: Worc	Strensham Rd. WR8: Naun, Rya
Sherwood La. WR2: Worc	Spa Ct. WR14: Mal	Stroma Av. WR5: Worc
Shetland Cl. WR3: Worc	Spa Rd. WR9: D Spa	Stuart Ri. WR5: Worc
Shipston Cl. WR4: Warn	Sparrowhawk Cl. WR14: Mal	Styles Ct. WR9: Omb
Shipwrights Cl. WR4: Worc	Spencer Dr. WR14: Mal	(off Sandys Rd.)
Shire Bus. Pk. WR4: Warn	Spencers Wlk. WR14: Mal	Sudeley Av. WR4: Warn
Shire Way WR9: D Spa	Spenser Rd. WR2: Worc	Sudeley Cl. WR14: Mal
Shirley Cl. WR14: Mal	SPETCHLEY	Sudgrove Cl. WR4: Warn
Shirley Jones Cl. WR9: D Spa	Spetchley Pk. Gdns.	Suffolk Dr. WR4: Warn
Shirley Rd. WR9: D Spa	Spetchley Rd. WR5: Worc	Suffolk Way WR9: D Spa
Shopping Cen., The WR11: Eves	Spindle Rd. WR14: Mal	Sugarloaf Cl. WR14: Mal
Shor St. WR11: Eves	Spinney, The WR2: C End	Summerfield Gdns. WR11: Hamp
Shoulton La. WR2: Hall	WR2: Worc	Summerfield Rd. WR14: Mal
Showell Cl. WR9: D Spa	Spinney Gro. WR11: Eves	Summer St. WR3: Worc
Showell Grn. WR9: D Spa	Spion Kop WR10: Pin	Sundew Cl. WR3: Clain
Showell Gro. WR9: D Spa	Sport Dyson Perrins	Sunnyside WR10: Per

Sunnyside Cl.—Vetch Fld. Av.

Sunnyside Cl. WR5: Kemp 5G 25
Sunnyside Pk. WR3: Clain 4G 13
Sunnyside Rd. WR1: Worc 2F 17
Sunrise WR14: Mal 6F 27
Sunshine Cl. HR8: Led 2A 42
Surman St. WR1: Worc 1D 4 (3F 17)
Swaledale Ct. WR4: Warn 1D 18
Swallow Cl. WR5: Worc 4H 21
Swallowfields WR4: Warn 3E 19
Swallow Pl. WR9: D Spa 4F 11
Swan Dr. WR9: D Spa 6F 9
Swan La. WR11: Eves 6D 36
Swanpool M. WR2: Worc 6A 4
Swanpool Wlk. WR2: Worc 6A 4 (6E 17)
Swans Reach *WR11: Eves* . . . . *6D 36* *(off Swan La.)*
Swan Theatre
Worcester . . . . **2B 4 (4E 17)**
SWINESHERD 6E 19
Swinesherd Way WR5: Worc 2C 22
Swinton Cl. WR2: Worc 1C 20
Swinton La. WR2: Worc 6C 16
Swinyard Rd. WR14: Mal 2C 26
Sycamore Av. WR11: Eves 3F 39
Sycamore Cl. WR14: Mal 2E 27
Sycamore Rd. WR4: Worc 2A 18
Sydney St. WR3: Worc 1F 17
Synehurst WR11: Bad 1B 40
Synehurst Av. WR11: Bad 1B 40
Synehurst Cres. WR11: Bad 1B 40
SYTCHAMPTON 1A 6

T

Tabor Gdns. WR14: Mal 4E 27
Tagwell Cl. WR9: D Spa 3F 11
Tagwell Gdns. WR9: D Spa 2E 11
Tagwell Grange WR9: D Spa 3F 11
Tagwell Rd. WR9: D Spa 2D 10
Talavera Rd. WR5: B Vill 5B 22
Tallow Hill WR5: Worc 3G 5 (4H 17)
Tamar Cl. WR5: Worc 4H 5 (5A 18)
Tamarisk Cl. WR3: Clain 2A 14
Tamar Pl. WR11: Eves 2F 39
Tamworth Av. WR4: Warn 1E 19
Tanglewood Hgts. WR14: Mal 4B 26
Tan Ho. La. WR2: R'ick 2A 20
Tanhouse La. WR14: Mal 1D 26
Tanners Cl. WR4: Worc 1B 18
Tannery M. WR1: Worc 5E 5
Tansy Cl. WR3: Clain 2A 14
WR5: Worc 5H 21
Tantallon Cl. WR4: Warn 1D 18
Tapenhall Rd. WR3: Fern H 3A 14
Target Cl. HR8: Led 2A 42
Tattersall WR4: Warn 4D 18
Tavern Orchard WR4: Warn 2D 18
Tay Av. WR5: Worc 3A 22
Taylor's Ct. WR1: Worc 2D 4
Taylors La. WR1: Worc 2D 4 (4F 17)
WR5: Kemp 6G 21
Tayson Way WR14: Mal 2D 26
Tearne St. WR2: Worc 3C 16
Teasel Cl. WR5: Worc 5H 21
Teasel Way WR3: Clain 2A 14
Teesdale Cl. WR9: D Spa 2A 10
Teeswater Cl. WR3: Worc 6A 14
Teme Av. WR14: Mal 1H 29
Teme Cres. WR9: D Spa 3B 10
Teme Rd. WR4: Warn 3A 18
Temeside Way WR2: Pow 4D 20
Teme Way HR8: Led 2A 42
Temperance St. WR1: Worc 5F 5 (5G 17)
Temple M. *WR11: Eves* . . . . *1D 38* *(off Littleworth St.)*
Ten Acres WR9: D Spa 4C 8
Tench Cl. WR5: Worc 4G 21
Tennis Wlk. WR1: Worc 1D 4 (3F 17)
Tennyson Cl. WR3: Worc 6G 13
Tennyson Dr. WR14: Mal 5E 27
Terrace Rd. WR10: Per, Pin 3A 34
Terrace Wlk. WR3: Worc 1G 5 (3H 17)
Terrill Ct. WR11: Eves 6D 36
Tetbury Dr. WR4: Warn 6C 14
Tewkesbury Rd. WR8: Holl G, Rya 2F 33
Thackholme WR4: Warn 2E 19
Thames Cl. WR5: Worc 5A 18
Thames Dr. WR9: D Spa 2A 10
Thatchers Cl. WR9: D Spa 4B 8
Thatchers Ct. WR9: D Spa 4B 8
Thatchers Grn. *WR9: D Spa* . . . . *3B 8* *(off Westwood Rd.)*
Thatchers Piece *WR9: D Spa* . . . . *4B 8* *(off Thatchers Cl.)*
Thatchers Pl. *WR9: D Spa* . . . . *3B 8* *(off Thatchers Way)*
Thatchers Way WR9: D Spa 4B 8
The . . . .
Names prefixed with 'The' for example 'The Avenue' are indexed under the main name such as 'Avenue, The'
Thetford Av. WR4: Warn 1F 19
Thirlmere Cl. WR4: Warn 1D 18
Thirlstane Rd. WR14: Mal 3D 28
Thistle Cl. WR3: Clain 2A 14
WR5: Worc 4H 21
Thistledown WR11: Eves 4C 38
Thomas Baxter Cl. WR1: Worc 6E 5 (6G 17)
Thomas Cl. HR8: Led 2A 42
WR3: Fern H 3A 14
Thomas Morris Ho. WR8: Upt Sev 4D 32
Thorn Av. WR4: Worc 1A 18
Thorneloe Ct. *WR1: Worc* . . . . *2E 17* *(off Barbourne Cres.)*
Thorneloe Rd. WR1: Worc 2E 17
Thorneloe Wlk. WR1: Worc 3E 17
Thorngrove Rd. WR14: Mal 1E 29
Thorn Lea WR11: Eves 3G 39
Thornley Cl. WR13: C Grn 4A 30
Three Cocks La. WR11: Off 2G 37
Three Counties Showground **1H 31**
Three Springs Rd. WR10: Per 6B 34
Three Springs Trad. Est.
WR5: Worc 4G 5 (5H 17)
Threshfield Dr. WR4: Warn 3C 18
Tibberton Rd. WR14: Mal 1E 29
Tiddesley Wood Nature Reserve **5A 34**
Tilley's All. HR8: Led 3C 42
Till St. WR3: Worc 2G 17
Timberdine Av. WR5: Worc 2G 21
Timberdine Barns WR5: Worc 4G 21
Timberdine Cl. WR5: Worc 2H 21
Timber Down WR10: Wick 6F 35
Timber La. WR10: Wick 6F 35
Timms Grn. WR12: Will 1H 41
Tintern Av. WR3: Worc 2H 17
Tiree Av. WR5: Worc 3A 22
Tiverton Cl. WR4: Warn 6D 14
Toftdale Grn. WR4: Warn 3D 18
TOLLADINE 4B 18
Tolladine Rd. WR4: Warn, Worc 2G 5 (4H 17)
Toll House Cl. WR2: R'ick 1A 20
Tollhouse Dr. WR2: Worc 4D 16
Topham Av. WR4: Warn 3D 18
Toronto Cl. WR2: Worc 3C 20
Torridon Wlk. WR5: Worc 3B 22
Toulouse Dr. WR5: B Vill 5B 22
Tourist Info. Cen.
Broadway **5G 41**
Droitwich Spa **6D 8**
Evesham **1D 38**
Great Malvern **1D 28**
Ledbury **3B 42**
Pershore **5D 34**
Upton upon Severn **3C 32**
Worcester . . . . **4D 4 (5F 17)**
Tower Hill WR9: D Spa 6E 9
Tower Rd. WR3: Worc 1E 17
Town Acres WR4: Warn 2D 18
Towneley WR4: Warn 4E 19
Townsend St. WR1: Worc 2E 17
Townsend Way WR14: Mal 2G 27
Traherne Cl. HR8: Led 5C 42
Treacle Nook WR4: Warn 2D 18
Treadwells Ct. *WR11: Eves* . . . . *1D 38* *(off Littleworth St.)*
Tredennyke Ho. *WR1: Worc* . . . . *2E 17* *(off Barbourne Cres.)*
Tredennyke M. *WR1: Worc* . . . . *2E 17* *(off Barbourne Ter.)*
Trefoil Cl. WR5: Worc 5H 21
WR14: Mal 2H 29
Trehearn Rd. WR9: D Spa 6F 9
Trelawney Cl. WR2: Worc 6D 16
Trench La. WR9: D'tead, Odd 4G 11
Trent Cl. WR9: D Spa 2B 10
Trent Rd. WR5: Worc 4B 18
Trevithick Cl. WR4: Warn 3E 19
Triangle, The WR5: Worc 6D 18
Trimnel Grn. *WR9: D Spa* . . . . *1B 10* *(off Celvestune Way)*
Trinity, The WR1: Worc 3E 5 (4G 17)
Trinity Cl. WR11: Eves 3E 39
Trinity Pas. WR1: Worc 4E 5 (5G 17)
Trinity Rd. WR14: Mal 5C 26
Trinity St. WR1: Worc 3E 5 (4G 17)
TROTSHILL 3D 18
Trotshill La. E. WR4: Warn 2E 19
Trotshill La. W. WR4: Warn 2D 18
Trotshill Way WR4: Warn 3F 19
Troutbeck Dr. WR4: Warn 2B 18
Trow Way WR5: Worc 2F 21
Truro Gdns. WR5: Worc 5C 18
Tudor Cl. WR14: Mal 3G 29
Tudor House Heritage & Education Cen.
. . . . **5E 5 (5G 17)**
Tudor House Museum, The **3C 32**
Tudor M. *HR8: Led* . . . . *3B 42* *(off The Homend)*
Tudor Way WR2: Worc 4A 16
Tudor Yd. HR8: Led 3B 42
Tuffrey Cl. WR3: Worc 1F 17
Tulip Dr. WR11: Eves 1G 39
TUNNEL HILL 4A 32
Tunnel Hill WR3: Worc 2H 17
WR4: Worc 2H 17
WR8: Upt Sev 5A 32
Turbary Av. WR4: Warn 2E 19
Turners Cl. WR4: Worc 1B 18
Turnpike Cl. WR2: Worc 4D 16
Turrall St. WR3: Worc 1F 17
Tutbury Row WR4: Warn 1F 19
Twarnley Ri. WR4: Warn 4D 18
Tweed Cl. WR5: Worc 5A 18
TWYFORD 2E 37
Twyford Golf Course **2D 36**
Tybridge St. WR2: Worc 5B 4 (5E 17)
Tyddesley Wood La. WR10: Per 6B 34
Tyndale WR4: Warn 3E 19
Tyne Cl. WR5: Worc 5A 18
Tyne Dr. WR11: Eves 2G 39
Tyning, The WR9: D Spa 2B 10
Tythe Rd. WR12: B'way 4G 41
Tything, The WR1: Worc 1D 4 (3F 17)
Tything Ct. WR1: Worc 1D 4

U

Ullswater Cl. WR4: Warn 2C 18
Ulverston Grn. WR4: Warn 2B 18
Union La. WR9: D Spa 6C 8
Union Pl. WR3: Worc 6E 13
Union St. WR1: Worc 5E 5 (5G 17)
University of Worcester
City Campus . . . . **2C 4 (4F 17)**
St John's Campus **4C 16**
UPHAMPTON 3A 6
Uphampton La. WR9: Uph, Omb 3A 6
Uplands Dr. WR14: Mal 4C 26
Up. Chase Rd. WR14: Mal 1F 29
UPPER COLWALL 6B 28
Up. Ferry La. WR2: C End 4C 24
Upperfields HR8: Led 2C 42
Upper Ground WR4: Warn 2D 18
Upperhall Cl. HR8: Led 3C 42
Up. Hall Est. HR8: Led 3C 42
Up. Hook Rd. WR8: Upt Sev 3A 32
UPPER HOWSELL 2D 26
Up. Howsell Rd. WR14: Mal 2D 26
Up. Park St. WR5: Worc 6G 5 (6H 17)
Upper Tything WR1: Worc 1C 4 (3F 17)
UPPER WELLAND 5F 31
Up. Welland Rd. WR14: Mal W 4E 31
UPPER WICK 2A 20
Up. Wick La. WR2: R'ick 1A 20
UPPER WYCHE 5C 28
Upton Gdns. WR8: Upt Sev 5D 32
Upton Rd. WR2: Pow, C End 6C 20
Upton Snodsbury Rd. WR10: Pin 1A 34
UPTON UPON SEVERN 3C 32
Upton upon Severn Heritage Cen. . . . . ***3C 32*** ***(off Church St.)***

V

Vale Bus. Pk. WR11: Eves 5F 39
Vale Cl. WR14: Mal 2C 26
Vale Ho. WR11: Eves 6E 37
Vale Link Way WR11: Eves 5F 39
Valentines Cl. WR9: D Spa 3F 11
Vale Pk. Bus. Cen. WR11: Eves 5E 39
Valley Wlk. *WR9: D Spa* . . . . *1B 10* *(off Valley Way)*
Valley Way WR9: D Spa 1B 10
Vancouver Cl. WR2: Worc 3C 20
Vandra Cl. WR14: Mal 2F 27
Vauxhall St. WR3: Worc 2H 17
Venture Bus. Pk. WR2: Worc 2E 21
Vernon Gro. WR9: D Spa 6C 8
Vernon Pk. Rd. WR2: Worc 6D 16
Vesta Tilley Ct. WR1: Worc 4F 5
Vetch Fld. Av. WR4: Warn 3D 18

58 A-Z Worcester

Vicarage Cl. WR2: Hall 4B 12
Vicarage Ct. WR1: Worc 4F 5
Vicarage La. WR3: Clain 1G 13
Vicar St. WR3: Worc 3H 17
Victoria Av. WR5: Worc 6H 5 (6H 17)
WR9: D Spa 2D 10
WR11: Eves 5D 36
Victoria Ct. WR14: Mal 5D 26
Victoria Institute WR1: Worc 2D 4
Victoria La. WR3: Worc 1E 17
Victoria Pk. Rd. WR14: Mal 3F 27
Victoria Pl. WR5: Worc 6G 5 (6H 17)
Victoria Rd. HR8: Led 4A 42
WR14: Mal 5D 26
Victoria Sq. WR9: D Spa 6D 8
Victoria St. WR3: Worc 1E 17
Victoria Ter. WR10: Per 4D 34
Victoria Wlk. WR14: Mal 4C 26
(North Hill Gdns.)
WR14: Mal 6D 26
(Victoria Rd.)
Viewfields WR5: Worc 4D 18
Vigornia Av. WR3: Worc 2G 17
Viking Way HR8: Led 2A 42
Village St. WR11: Ald 1A 40
Villa Way HR8: Led 5B 42
Vimiera Cl. WR5: B Vill 5B 22
Vincent Rd. WR5: Worc 5G 5 (5H 17)
Vine M. WR11: Eves 1D 38
VINES, THE 5D 8
Vines La. WR9: D Spa 5D 8
(not continuous)
Vines M. WR9: D Spa 5D 8
Vine St. WR3: Worc 6F 13
WR11: Eves 1D 38
Vintners Cl. WR4: Worc 1B 18
Viscount Cobham Ct. WR14: Mal 5F 27
Vivian Av. WR2: R'ick 1A 20
Vue Cinema
Worcester 5E 5 (5G 17)

W

Wadborough Rd. WR5: Nort 6E 23
Wadley Dr. WR3: Worc 3E 13
Waggon Pl. WR4: Warn 2D 18
Wain Grn. WR4: Warn 2D 18
Wainwright Rd. WR4: Warn 5D 14
Wakefield Cl. WR5: Worc 5B 18
Wakeman St. WR3: Worc 1F 17
WALCOT 1C 34
Walcot Rd. WR10: D Bro, Per 1D 34
Walkers La. WR3: Whitt 1C 12
Walkers Way WR5: Worc 2C 22
Walkmill Dr. WR9: Wych 1H 9
Walkworth Av. WR4: Warn 1E 19
Wallcroft Cl. WR2: Worc 3C 16
Walled Garden, The HR8: Led 4C 42
Walmer Cres. WR4: Warn 6E 15
Walnut Av. WR4: Worc 2B 18
Walnut Cl. WR12: B'way 5F 41
Walnut Cres. WR14: Mal W 5D 28
Walnut Tree M. WR5: Worc 6G 5
Walsgrove Cl. WR1: Worc 2C 4
Wolwyn Rd WR13: C Grn, C Sto, Upp C . . .3A 30
Wardour Pl. WR4: Warn 2E 19
Wards Cl. WR11: Eves 2G 39
Warmstry Ct. WR1: Worc 4C 4
WARNDON .1C 18
Warndon Bus. Pk. WR4: Warn 5C 14
Warndon Grn. WR4: Warn 5B 18
Warndon La. WR4: Warn 1F 19
Warndon Way WR4: Warn 6G 15
Warndon Woods (Local Nature Reserve) . . .2F 19
Warren Dr. HR8: Led 4C 42
Warriors Way WR3: Hind 5G 15
Warwick Ct. WR14: Mal 1C 28
Wasdale Ct. WR4: Warn 6B 14
Waseley Cl. WR5: Worc 4A 22
Washbrook Cl. WR4: Warn 6D 14
Washington Rd. WR11: W'ford 5B 40
Washington St. WR1: Worc 1E 5 (3G 17)
Washpole La. WR9: New 6F 11
Wassage Ct. WR9: Hamp L 2B 8
Wassage Way WR9: Hamp L 2B 8
Wassage Way Nth. WR9: Hamp L 2A 8
Wassage Way Sth. WR9: Hamp L 2A 8
Watchetts Grn. WR4: Warn 3E 19
Water Cft. WR4: Warn 2D 18
Waterford Cl. WR3: Worc 6E 13
Waterloo Cl. WR13: Mad 3H 27
Waterloo Ho. WR1: Worc 1E 5 (3G 17)
Waters Edge WR1: Worc 1F 21
(off Armstrong Dr.)

Waterside WR8: Upt Sev 3C 32
WR9: D Spa 6E 9
WR11: Eves 2D 38
Waterside Cl. WR9: D Spa 5E 9
Waterside Ho. WR8: Upt Sev 3C 32
(off Waterside)
Waterside Pk. Caravan Site WR4: Warn 5E 15
Waters Reach WR1: Worc 1F 21
(off Armstrong Dr.)
Waterworks Rd. WR1: Worc 2E 17
WR3: Worc 2E 17
Waterworks Wlk. WR1: Worc 1E 17
Watery La. WR2: Worc 6C 16
WR11: Hamp 2A 38
WR14: L Mal 6F 31
Watkins Way WR14: Mal 2G 29
Watsons La. WR11: Eves 2E 39
Waveney Rd. WR9: D Spa 2B 10
Waverley St. WR5: Worc 2G 21
Weaver Cl. WR9: D Spa 6F 9
Weavers Ct. WR3: Worc 5F 13
Webb Dr. WR9: Wych 2E 9
Wedderburn Rd. WR14: Mal 1G 29
Wedgeberrow Rd. WR9: D Spa 1D 10
Wedley Pl. WR4: Warn 4E 19
Weir Gdns. WR10: Per 5E 35
Weir La. WR2: Worc 2E 21
Weir Meadow Caravan Pk.
WR11: Eves 6E 37
WELLAND .4H 31
Welland Cl. WR9: D Spa 2B 10
Welland Gdns. WR13: Well 4G 31
Welland Rd. WR8: Upt Sev 5A 32
Wellesley Ct. WR9: D Spa 6D 16
Wellington Cl. WR1: Worc 4F 5 (5G 17)
Wellington Rd. WR9: Omb 4A 6
Wells Cl. WR14: Mal W 4E 31
Wells Gdns. WR12: B'way 5H 41
Wells Rd. WR5: Worc 5C 18
WR14: Mal, Mal W 4C 28
Wensleydale WR9: D Spa 2B 10
Wensleydale Dr. WR3: Worc 6A 14
Wentworth Ct. WR3: Worc 1F 17
Werstan Cl. WR14: Mal 2G 29
Wessex Rd. WR14: Mal 2G 27
WESTACRE .5C 8
West Bank WR9: D Spa 4C 8
Westbourne Cl. WR2: Worc 3A 4 (4D 16)
Westbury Av. WR9: D Spa 2A 10
Westbury Ct. WR9: D Spa 2A 10
(off New Chawson La.)
Westbury St. WR1: Worc 1F 5 (3G 17)
Westcroft Ct. WR9: D Spa 6C 8
(off Ombersley Way)
Westcroft St. WR9: D Spa 6D 8
WEST END .6F 41
West End La. WR12: B'way 6E 41
Westfield Cl. WR3: Fern H 2B 14
Westfield Rd. WR3: Fern H 2A 14
Westhaven Pl. WR2: Worc 2C 16
WESTLANDS 4B 8
Westlands WR9: D Spa 5B 8
Westlea Cl. WR9: D Spa 6B 16
Westlyn Cl. WR14: Mal 4F 27
WEST MALVERN 6A 26
W. Malvern Rd. WR14: Mal, W Mal 5A 26
Westmead Cl. WR9: D Spa 6C 8
Westminster Bank WR14: W Mal 6A 26
Westminster Rd. WR5: Worc 5B 18
WR14: Mal W 5C 28
Westmount Cl. WR2: Worc 3C 20
Westonbirt Cl. WR5: Worc 4A 22
West Pk. Dr. WR9: D Spa 5B 8
West Stone WR9: D Spa 3C 8
West St. WR9: D Spa 6C 8
WR11: Eves 1C 38
Westview Cl. WR2: Worc 5B 16
Westward Rd. WR14: Mal 1C 26
Westwood Av. WR9: D Spa 2D 10
Westwood Cl. WR9: D Spa 1A 10
Westwood Ho. WR9: Westw 5G 7
WESTWOOD PARK 5H 7
Westwood Rd. WR9: D Spa 5B 8
Westwood Way WR9: D Spa 6H 7
Weyburn Rd. WR2: Worc 3C 20
Wey Cl. WR9: D Spa 1B 10
Wey Pl. WR9: D Spa 1B 10
(off Wey Cl.)
Wharf, The WR1: Worc 1G 21
Wharfedale Cres. WR9: D Spa 2A 10
Wharfedale Dr. WR4: Warn 3C 18
Wharf Ho. WR1: Worc 2F 5
Wheatfield Av. WR5: Worc 4G 21
Wheatfields Pk. Est. WR2: C End 2D 24
Wheatley La. WR8: Upt Sev 6A 32

Wheeler Cl. WR2: Worc 4A 4 (5D 16)
Wheelwright Cl. WR4: Worc 1B 18
Whinfield Gdns. WR5: Worc 4F 13
Whinfield Rd. WR3: Worc 4F 13
Whitakers Cl. WR10: Per 4D 34
Whitborn Cl. WR14: Mal 1G 29
Whitborn End WR14: Mal 1G 29
Whitcroft Rd. WR10: Per 4D 34
White Castle WR4: Warn 1E 19
Whitehall Cl. WR2: R'ick 1A 20
White Hill WR4: Warn 3C 18
Whitehorse Cl. WR4: Warn 3C 20
White Ladies Cl. WR1: Worc 3F 17
White Ladies Wlk. WR1: Worc 3F 17
Whites Ct. WR2: Worc 2D 20
Whites Rd. WR2: Worc 2E 21
Whitethorn Gro. WR14: Mal 4G 27
Whitewood Cl. WR5: Worc 2C 22
Whitewood Way WR5: Worc 1C 22
Whitmore Rd. WR2: Worc 6B 16
Whittingham Cl. WR9: D Spa 6D 8
Whittingham Ho. WR9: D Spa 6E 9
(off Worcester Rd.)
WHITTINGTON 2D 22
Whittington Ga. WR5: Worc 1B 22
Whittington Rd. WR5: Worc 1C 22
WICK 6F 35
Wickham Cl. WR11: W'ford 5B 40
WICKHAMFORD 5B 40
Wickhamford La. WR11: Eves, W'ford 3G 39
Wick Ho. Cl. WR10: Wick 6F 35
Wigton Pl. WR4: Warn 2B 18
Wilberforce Pl. WR4: Warn 4E 19
Wildwood Dr. WR5: Worc 6D 18
Wilfred Ct. WR3: Worc 2G 17
WILLERSEY .1H 41
Willersey Ind. Est. WR12: Will 1H 41
Willersey Rd. WR11: Bad 3C 40
Willets Rd. WR9: D Spa 3D 10
William Cres. WR11: Eves 1C 38
William Ho. WR1: Eves 5D 36
(off St Christopher Ct.)
Williams Ct. WR14: Mal 6G 27
(off Burrows Cl.)
William Shakespeare Pl. WR9: D Spa 3D 10
Williamson Rd. WR5: Worc 4H 5 (4H 17)
William Tennant Way WR8: Upt Sev 5D 32
Willow Bank WR10: W Pid 1G 35
Willow Cl. WR3: Fern H 2C 14
WR8: Rya 3F 33
WR10: Per 4C 34
WR10: Pin 2B 34
Willow Ct. WR5: Worc 4G 5 (5H 17)
WR9: D Spa 5B 8
Willow Dr. WR9: D Spa 3D 10
Willow Gro. WR14: Mal 4E 27
Willow Rd. WR11: Eves 3F 39
WR12: Will 2H 41
Willowslea Rd. WR3: Worc 4E 13
Willow St. WR1: Worc 6G 17
Walnut Rd. WR14: Mal 2D 26
Wilson St. WR3: Worc 1G 5 (3H 17)
Wilton Rd. WR14: Mal 1F 29
Winchcombe Dr. WR4: Warn 6B 14
Winchester Av. WR4: Warn 1D 20
Windermere Dr. WR4: Warn 6B 14
Windles Row WR4: Warn 2D 18
Windmeres WR11: Eves 2F 39
Windmill Cl. WR1: Worc 3F 17
Windmill Cotts. WR3: Clain 1A 14
Windmill La. WR5: Kemp 3G 25
Windrush Cl. WR5: Worc 5A 18
Windrush Cres. WR14: Mal 1H 29
Windsor Av. WR4: Worc 5C 16
Windsor Cl. WR14: Mal 1G 27
Windsor Rd. WR9: D Spa 3D 10
WR11: Eves 5E 37
Windsor Row WR1: Worc 4E 5 (5G 17)
Wingfield Av. WR4: Warn 1E 19
Winnetts La. WR9: D Spa 6D 8
Winnings, The WR13: C Sto 6A 28
Winnipeg Cl. WR2: Worc 3C 20
Winslow Av. WR9: D Spa 6F 9
Winsmore WR2: Pow 6C 20
Winston Cl. HR8: Led 5C 42
Winterburn Rd. WR2: Worc 1C 16
Wirlpiece Av. WR4: Warn 2E 19
Wiselack Pl. WR4: Warn 3D 18
Wisteria Dr. WR11: Eves 1G 39
Withinbrook Rd. WR2: Worc 6E 17
Withincroft Cl. WR4: Warn 3D 18
Witney Ct. WR4: Warn 6C 14
WITTON 1D 10
Witton Av. WR9: D Spa 2B 10
Wolsey Cl. WR4: Worc 4A 18

Wolverton Rd. WR1: Worc 1F **5** (3G **17**)
Woodbine Rd. WR1: Worc 2E **17**
Woodbridge Cl. WR5: Worc 3H **21**
Woodbury La. WR5: Nort 6E **23**
Woodbury Pk. WR5: Nort 6F **23**
Woodbury Ri. WR14: Mal 3C **26**
Wood End WR11: Eves 4E **39**
Woodfarm Rd. WR14: Mal W 1F **31**
Woodfield La. WR9: Omb 1A **6**
Woodfield Rd. HR8: Led 5B **42**
    WR9: D Spa .5E **9**
Woodfields WR9: D Spa 5E **9**
WOODGREEN .2E **19**
Woodgreen Dr. WR4: Warn 6D **14**
Woodhall Cl. WR9: Omb 4A **6**
Woodhall Ct. WR9: Omb 4A **6**
Woodhall La. WR9: Omb 4A **6**
Woodhouse Cl. WR5: Worc 1F **21**
Woodland Cl. WR3: Worc 1H **17**
Woodland Cotts. WR1: Worc 1E **5**
Woodland Piece WR11: Eves 4F **39**
Woodland Rd. WR3: Worc 1H **17**
Woodlands WR11: Eves 4E **39**
Woodlands, The WR8: Rya 3E **33**
Woodlands Cl. WR14: Mal 4E **31**
Wood Leason Av. WR4: Warn 2D **18**
Woodleigh Cl. HR8: Led 3B **42**
Woodleigh Rd. HR8: Led 3B **42**
Woodmancote WR4: Warn 6B **14**
Woodmans Cl. WR9: D Spa 4B **8**
    (off Woodmans Way)
Woodmans Grn. WR9: D Spa 5B **8**
Woodmans Pl. WR9: D Spa 5B **8**
    (off Farriers Cl.)
Woodmans Ri. WR9: D Spa 4B **8**
Woodmans Way WR9: D Spa 4B **8**
Wood Piece Cl. WR4: Warn 6D **14**
Woodrow Ho's. WR9: D Spa 6E **9**
Woodshears All. WR14: Mal 2D **28**
Woodshears Dr. WR14: Mal 2E **29**
Woodshears Rd. WR14: Mal 2D **28**
Woodside La. WR13: Well 3H **31**
Woodside Rd. WR5: Worc 6A **18**
Woodstock Rd. WR2: Worc 4C **16**
Wood Ter. WR1: Worc 1D **4** (3F **17**)
    WR10: Per 6C **34**
Woodward Cl. WR10: Per 6C **34**

Woodward Rd. WR10: Per 6C **34**
Woolhope Ri. WR5: Worc 1G **21**
Woolhope Rd. WR5: Worc 6G **17**
Woolmead Row WR4: Warn 2F **19**
Worboys Rd. WR2: Worc 1D **20**
WORCESTER 4D **4** (5F **17**)
Worcester Cathedral 5D **4** (5F **17**)
Worcester Citizens' Swimming Pool 3E **21**
Worcester City FC 2F **17**
Worcester Countryside Cen. 6D **18**
Worcester Crematorium WR3: Worc 1H **17**
Worcester Foregate Street Station (Rail)
    . . . . .3D **4** (4F **17**)
Worcester Golf Course 1C **20**
Worcester Golf Range 3F **21**
Worcester Norton Sports Cen. 5B **22**
Worcester Porcelain Mus. 6E **5** (6G **17**)
Worcester Racecourse 2B **4** (3E **17**)
Worcester Rd. HR8: Led 3C **42**
    WR5: Worc .5G **21**
    WR8: E Cro .1E **33**
    WR9: D Spa .3C **10**
    WR9: Wych 2E **9**
    WR10: Per 4C **34**
    WR10: W Pid 1G **35**
    WR11: Eves .3B **36**
    WR13: New .1H **27**
    WR14: Mal 6C **26**
Worcester RUFC 6F **15**
Worcestershire, The WR9: D Spa 6D **8**
Worcestershire County Cricket Club
    . . . . .5C **4** (6E **17**)
Worcestershire Golf Course 6D **28**
Worcestershire Masonic Library & Mus.
    . . . . .1F **5** (3G **17**)
WORCESTERSHIRE ROYAL HOSPITAL 5D **18**
Worcester Shrub Hill Station (Rail)
    . . . . .3H **5** (4H **17**)
Worcester Sports Arena 4B **4** (5E **17**)
Worcester Swimming Pool & Fitness Cen.
    . . . . .1E **5** (3G **17**)
Worcester Trade Pk.
    WR4: Worc 2H **5** (4A **18**)
Worcester Trad. Est. WR3: Worc 6A **14**
Worcester Woods Country Pk. 6C **18**
Wordsworth Av. WR3: Worc 1G **17**
Wordsworth Grn. WR14: Mal 5E **27**

Workman Rd. WR11: Hamp 2B **38**
Worthington Gdns. WR4: Warn 3E **19**
Wren Av. WR14: Mal 5G **27**
Wren Cl. WR3: Clain 2A **14**
Wryflatt WR4: Warn 2E **19**
Wyatts M. WR1: Worc 5E **5**
WYCHBOLD 2E **9**
Wych Elm Cl. WR5: Worc 1A **22**
Wyche Rd. WR14: Mal W 5B **28**
Wych Rd. WR9: D Spa 1C **10**
Wye Av. WR14: Mal 1H **29**
Wye Cl. WR5: Worc 4H **5** (5A **18**)
    WR9: D Spa .3C **10**
Wye Vw. HR8: Led 2A **42**
Wykewane WR14: Mal 2H **29**
Wyld's La. WR5: Worc 6F **5** (6G **17**)
Wyre Hill WR10: W Pid 1F **35**
WYRE PIDDLE .1G **35**
Wyre Piddle By-Pass
    WR10: Pin, Upp M 3B **34**
Wyre Rd. WR10: Per 2E **35**

Y

Yarrow Cl. WR5: Worc 5H **21**
Yates Hay Rd. WR14: Mal 2D **26**
Yeoman Cl. HR8: Led 1A **42**
Yewleigh La. WR8: Upt Sev 5A **32**
Yew Tree Cl. WR5: Worc 1B **22**
    WR11: Eves .3F **39**
Yewtree Cl. WR13: C Grn 4A **30**
Yew Tree Ct. WR5: B Vill 5A **22**
Yew Tree Hill WR9: D Spa 3D **10**
Yew Tree La. WR3: Fern H 2C **14**
    WR14: Mal W 4F **31**
Yock La. WR10: Wick 5F **35**
York Av. WR9: D Spa 2D **10**
York Cl. WR14: Mal 1F **27**
York Pl. WR1: Worc 1C **4** (3E **17**)
York Pl. La. WR1: Worc 1B **4** (3E **17**)

Z

Zermatt Cl. WR3: Worc 5E **13**
Zetland Rd. WR14: Mal 5D **26**

SAFETY CAMERA INFORMATION

Safety camera locations are publicised by the Safer Roads Partnership which operates them in order to encourage drivers to comply with speed limits at these sites. It is the driver's absolute responsibility to be aware of and to adhere to speed limits at all times.

By showing this safety camera information it is the intention of Geographers' A-Z Map Company Ltd., to encourage safe driving and greater awareness of speed limits and vehicle speed. Data accurate at time of printing.

Printed and bound in the United Kingdom by Gemini Press Ltd., Shoreham-by-Sea, West Sussex
Printed on materials from a sustainable source